I have ingested this memoir as one whole story–it is profoundly moving. Angel is a marvelous storyteller and a skilled word-crafter. The rhythm of her sentences carries me along. Her language is vivid, specific, full of flavor, image-rich. This candid telling is the first memoir I've read about growing up as a child of alcoholics. The details, the repetitions of behaviors, the feelings and coping mechanisms…I love this book. It is so, so brave.

—Leiah Bowden, artist and author of
Amidah in the Pandemic: Received Blessings

Angel Booth has accomplished something remarkable with her new book *Sober Thoughts: a memoir/alcoholism, family, courage and redemption.* By sharing with us the impact of growing up with an alcoholic mother, she has opened a window for us to look through to see what it's like to suffer the paradox of living with alcoholism.

She tells us … "My mother was one of the kindest people I have ever known, and she abandoned us all for her daily drinking. She could be rational, cautious and caring, and she put us at risk many times because she was drunk…she was maddening to live with, yet we loved her. This is the crazy-making, human complexity of alcoholism."

This book is a must read for anyone living with the difficulty of addiction, either personally or with loved ones. The book contains many references that can be followed for help and support.

— Gary Sherman, Psychotherapist, teacher and author of
Tales of a Committed Visitor: Living and Learning as Spirit in Form.

Cover photo: Bruce Gibbs, PhD.

The image in the center of the tray is my mother, who posed for an artist who sold to Coca Cola. The image is from 1937, American Artworks, Inc. In its day, in all of the US but the coasts, women's bathing suits still came down to their knees. Because this image, with suit ending at the hip crease, was considered "racy" by most of the country and was rejected by many businesses and magazines refused to use it in the ads, it became (naturally) the most popular tray of its day.

Sobering Thoughts

a memoir

alcoholism, family, courage and redemption

Angel Booth

Paperback ISBN: 979-8-89121-893-2

Ebook ISBN: 979-8-89121-892-5

Library of Congress Number:

Cover photo: Bruce Gibbs

Interior Design: Leo Baquero

Sobering Thoughts by Angel Weatherly Booth, 2024

Sobering Thoughts Blog at Wordpress.com

https://soberingthoughtsdotorg.wordpress.com

Printed in the United States of America

I dedicate this "grimoire" to sober alcoholics, ACA's, Al-Anon's, and anyone trying to live a better life despite the load of confusion and grief from alcoholism in the family. And, to young ones who may look to use alcohol for getting happy, getting high, getting ready, getting you through, getting going, or getting anything but in your right minds. Maybe this book will help you, through my story and what I've learned, and through exposure to the truth and the lie about the disease of alcoholism, to make better decisions to survive and thrive.

"I have been in Sorrow's kitchen and licked out all the pots. Then I have stood on the peaky mountain wrapped in rainbows, with a harp and sword in my hands."

—Zora Neale Hurston

Table of Contents

"Alcohol is God's apology
for making us self-aware."

—Author unknown

Acknowledgements

I wish to thank the following people for helping me give the proper emotional "shape" and "shade" to this memoir: Authors Lynn Lowery, Southeast 37th Street, and Leiah Bowden, artist/author, Amidah in the Pandemic: Received Blessings, both for their thorough and thoughtful diving into this memoir. In their own ways, they each helped me find a thread of integrity to pull on. Also, Korie Shokmalli, RN, BA, Holistic Healer and Teacher, and long, long time friend and mentor, for her passionate and compassionate read on this text. I thank the Friday afternoon writers group: Jan Ogren, MFT, Jo Lauer, MFT, Robin Zolotoff, Jing Li, and Heather Smith, for faithfully reading and giving me excellent feedback and direction. Lastly, for the love, support and photographic help from my husband, Bruce Gibbs, PhD, thank you for believing in me!

One last note: this memoir gained support (as I did) from years of attending Al-Anon. Many listeners in the Al-Anon rooms have helped me articulate my experience of being a Child of Alcoholic parents by their careful listening and by generously sharing their own lives.

Introduction

SOBERING THOUGHTS IS SLICE OF MY LIFE showing the humor and horror of living with alcoholics. And a little about how I (eventually) moved toward healing and freedom. If you grew up with alcoholics in your family, you may or may not be aware that there is not only denial in the alcoholic, but denial in the children of alcoholics. You will not leave it all behind you as you grow up and move into your life and relationships. Denial lives *in* you, tints the lenses covering your inward eyes, and blinds you to pain and damage left inside. The effects of alcoholism in the family last more than a lifetime. They are passed down to your children even if you, yourself, did not become an alcoholic. More than any other wish I could wish, or hope I could hope, I wish and hope that my experiences, realizations and stories will make you more aware of the beliefs and conclusions you have made about life, about *your* life, that have their origins in the disease of alcoholism. And, by opening to greater awareness, you, too, will move toward healing and freedom.

Sobering Thoughts begins with my memoir about a period in my life where I began to awaken to my mother's alcoholism and its effects upon me and my family. In the memories I share of her, expect an untidy mix of humor and horror, as *is* life with alcoholics. Through the writing process I re-discovered the *language of drinking*, and have enjoyed finding and remembering the courageous transformations I have witnessed in people affected by this disease.

There are memories my brother, sister and I reflect upon with shuddering horror or disgust; others we hold in high amusement. The line between horror and humor can be paper thin when living with an alcoholic. As we three kids grew up, we used the family-style ironic humor with snide commentary to hide our shame and powerlessness. As we grew older, our reflections sound sardonic, and bitter. Together, we exaggerate our tales from sublimely inane to ridiculous extremes by recalling our mother's stupid antics, drinking-thinking, deep denial and clever justifications for her addiction. At times we are somber, incredulous; other times reduced to belly shaking laughter, tears streaming down our faces, all propriety annihilated by the perfect madness of our life with Mother. We rarely doubted her love for us, but daily called into question the choices she made that made her life and ours feel out of control.

I hope these stories will reach into your life, especially if you need to consider if you are at risk for *becoming* addicted. Or, you may be a young person and might need to know you are not crazy though you may live in an insane family *system* fueled by alcohol. Maybe this memoir can help change a life trajectory. Life is full of possibilities, and sometimes you need to know that it is possible to live differently, to recover from the insanity of alcoholism, create and move toward what you want, and *be* the person you know you are capable of being.

This book began with collaboration in mind. I interviewed sober alcoholics, I read articles and memoirs, I trolled the net for ideas and people I would like to interview trying to create some momentum. Not too far into the process, people stopped volunteering to interview and I stopped asking. Instead, I wrote. I composed essays I thought had nothing to do with *Sobering Thoughts*—just memories I felt inspired to capture. My writing files were disorganized and poorly documented—a scatter of ideas and barely conceived "chapters" of I knew not what. Years flew by. Other writing priorities sailed to the top of the list and *Sobering Thoughts* became a mere idea that might never be fully manifested.

In 2013 my beloved niece, Emily, died in a car crash of her own making, died in a drunken stupor, died alone but for the young man in the car she hit head-on. It was not the first time she drove drunk, nor was her lack of sobriety a surprise to her family. She left behind a legacy of addiction, pain, loss, violence and brokenness, recovery, reconciliations and relapses. You might expect me to say that Emily's death galvanized in me a writing fury to tell our tales and offer some sense to young people who drink. I wish it had.

Her death was a tremendous shock and the waves of horror and grief that followed knocked me down for months. All the more so because we had become so close in the last few years before her death, and it seemed that she had finally been able to stay sober for more than two years. We celebrated, we laughed and cried together, we shared our childhood stories and laughed and cried some more. We revealed our healing experiences and shared advice.

Unknown to me at the time, in some way our relationship had become for Emily another sham of addiction—the old poison speaking through her soul, and the poison of my denial about alcoholics, causing me to perceive what I most wanted to hear. In fact, I had become one more person in Emily's life she had to lie to, one more anchor she would reach out for, to help her hold the fantasy of sobriety, her valence of "normal" in life and relationships. In truth she rarely stayed sober for more than a few months.

Sobering Thoughts opens with Emily's story as prologue, my account of some of her life and the non-ordinary events surrounding her departure from it. Years have flown by since her death and it is high time to gather up the bits and scraps of relevant writing, the seeming disparate chunks calling to each other and me, to pull it together and put it down once and for all.

Don't worry about the strange things I describe about Emily's passing and after. Read it as an actual account, I am not making up a story here. The scenarios I describe may or may not be outside your scope of experience, interest or belief. Suffice it to say, none of us has a handle on any particular reality. We are multi-dimensional beings and we create multi-layered dimensions of reality to live and to grow within.

In Part I the chapters begin with a string of memories of life with my alcoholic mother and some sobering realizations occurring on our six-month driving tour of the U.S. and resettlement in Virginia. During this trip I began to awaken to the truth of my mother's drinking and the effects upon us three kids. I began to notice my embarrassment in public and feel the rage and shame of being powerless while she was "Drunk and Disorderly."

In the "Denial" chapter, there are other people's stories as well—all real accounts, with not much punching up to make them more funny/awful. The circumstances and thinking process of the alcoholics involved says it all.

Part II begins with my personal awakening stories: what I have learned about myself in relationships that reflected life with my alcoholic mother; bits about being a child of an alcoholic and setting boundaries; dry drunk behavior; finding the courage to change; my brush with drugs; a few things I have learned and practiced that we can call "self-help" for want of a better term.

Part III is "Resources for Living with Alcoholism" and contains some essays and information about Al-Anon and my experiences in Al-Anon; some real life (and death) numbers to consider from Mothers Against Drunk Driving and other sources; relevant quotes and tidbits from or about famous drunks, a few articles about alcohol from the local newspaper, a few Darwin Award stories to keep it chipper, and a smattering of grim statistics to bring you back to your senses.

Enjoy. Consider. Pass the book along to others: You can't throw a stone in any community without hitting an alcoholic or someone affected by the disease.

Family Portrait

I feel the need to paint a few word pictures of my parents in order for you to see more clearly the ideas and images I hold about them. And, to illustrate their lives a little, from the stories I heard them tell and from my own experiences as their child.

About Mother: You will read in later chapters something of her "other side" or the more shining attributes, talents and character she also possessed and displayed. Alcoholics are not one-dimensional beings. Mother's first drink often brought forth, or made evident, her caring and compassion and even wisdom. That initial lifting of inhibitions helped her feel free and undistorted. But alcoholics do not stop after the first drink. Or the second, or the third. And so the brief feeling of clarity and openness my mother might display degraded quickly as she drank, and she became massively distorted in thinking and being, aggrandized, all proportion lost.

She was born Doris Weatherly Westall, from a "fine, old Southern family." One older sister, Emily, and an older brother, Billy. My grandmother had another boy, before Mother, named Jimmy. He died in infancy (Mother was to also have a son, who died in infancy, also named Jimmy). Doris was a sensitive tom-boy in her youth, tall and thin, a tree-climber, who later became an athlete and elegant model of fine clothes.

Her parents divorced when Doris was 12. Her father, Henry, was often remiss in alimony and child support so Doris had to go to her grandfather and ask for the money. Grandpa Westall lectured young Doris about the "leeches on my back" while he drove a grand touring car and lived "high on the hog" as we say in the South. These episodes tended to crush what little self-esteem she had.

I believe my Grandpa Henry and his father were both alcoholics and bullies. My great grandfather's inheritance dissolved to nothing in the Reconstruction period following the Civil War. Property and slaves gone. Nothing but a "good name" and bitterness to pass on to his sons. My grandmothers' parents were not heavy drinkers, though that lineage does boast of several notable alcoholics in its past. That line of family also owned property and slaves, and came out of the Civil War with only their names to recommend them.

Doris met Bill (my father) in the Navy in 1944 or 45. She was a sharp shooter, and very good at math, so the Navy put her to work teaching the men how to fire everything from small arms to the big anti-aircraft guns on battleships. Bill was in one of her classes. He had been in the Navy since he was seventeen, mostly serving on unarmed supply ships running food, ammunition and other needful things to the coast of England from Reykjavik, Iceland. He had seen some horrible sights at sea, the result of German U-Boat torpedoes destroying allied ships, and was, like many, traumatized. He had come home to the states to learn artillery while his ship was being outfitted with anti-aircraft guns. He considered himself a career Navy man by then, as was his father.

Dad and Mother dated maybe three times before he proposed. Dad reluctantly left the service shortly after the end of the war to take care of his new wife and their first child, born in early March of 1946. Each attended the University of Virginia, school of architecture and engineering, but never finished their degrees. Dad liked to say he would have "$10,000.00 next week" with many of his schemes. He was certain he could make a fortune in California in the post-war building boom, so he built our home there and sent for Mother and my sister and brother in 1949.

In the Navy, Dad had been injured but not treated for concussion and brain trauma. Within a year of their marriage he began to exhibit signs of mental illness—paranoia, unreasonable anger and fear, severe headaches. He threatened Mother. His threats over time escalated into fights and violence. He tried to kill her three times, she would later recall, the last time in California when she was pregnant with me. My sister interrupted him in the act so he grabbed my brother, then about eighteen months old, and drove out to his mother's house in the desert.

My dad's father, Howard, a retired Navy commander, assisted my mom in having my dad committed to Camarillo State Mental Hospital when I was three months old. He was diagnosed paranoid-schizophrenic. My father learned to "behave" at Camarillo, and to recognize when he needed treatment. If he got in trouble with people or the law and did not go back to the hospital and turn himself in, he faced more insulin and/or electro-shock therapy to help him accept his condition. Mother had to face raising three kids and keeping up the house payments on her own. They had been together less than five years.

In my mother's family there were many alcoholics, probably more than I know of. Her father and grandfather for starters. My mother's brother, Unc, and sister, Emily, were alcoholics too, though my aunt and her husband rarely drank in public, and rarely drank to excess. They simply drank every day, many highballs apiece beginning at about five and ending around ten.

My father's family boasted numbers of alcoholics. Excluding his mother, my Grandma Jen, who likely never had more than the occasional glass of sherry, my granddad Howard drank heavily and died relatively young. Both my aunts and one of my two uncles drank daily to excess, as did their spouses. My dads' younger brother, non-drinking Uncle John, may have been saved by his uber-religious teetotaling wife. I know of at least one cousin who is an alcoholic (there are very likely more). Though I don't believe I ever witnessed drunkenness in my father, he was known to "put away a lot of beer." Both parents smoked like chimneys.

My Grandma Jen saw only the positive in everyone. When my mother tried to tell her about how violent my dad could be, she replied to my mother that Bill could be a "little moody" and was like that as a child. His sisters told me that Grandma Jen would send Dad to his room for some "rude behavior" and Dad might not come out for several days or a week. They thought he had always been a little off and the war made him worse.

All I knew about my parents until I was ten was that they were only partly engaged in their (and my) lives. I was rarely able to attract my mother's attention for very long, partly because my older brother and sister commanded more of her much of the time. But by age ten I began to know without a doubt the link between alcohol and my mother's lack of presence. By thirteen, I could see that alcohol was her world, in spite of the fact that she loved me or seemed sometimes to care about what I experienced. In my later teen years, I was mostly angry about her addiction and shamed by her behavior. Her ability to demonstrate her love and caring was hampered by alcohol, and her daily drinking kept her focused on her own pain. By twenty-two I also came to understand she did not have, perhaps never had, any room inside for anyone else's experience or pain, her own pain being all-consuming of her energy. But I still did not connect this awareness to my own anxious feelings, to my anger and inability to move my life in a satisfying direction, for years to come.

Throughout my childhood I felt lonely, alone, abandoned and somehow wrong. My best companions for a time were a group of beings (not in bodies) who often hung out around me: an older, bearded man to my right, and behind him a group of beings I could not see but I could sense and sometimes hear. They listened to my thoughts and internal discoveries, and celebrated with each other when I gained a small understanding of a word or of a person or something in the world. They often clapped and got excited when I shared some new understanding. I came to regard the experience with these beings not as mental illness but as a sign that the universe was larger than my family, and I just might be special, worthy in some way.

As loneliness moved more deeply in, the feelings seemed to expand. I began to live in a world of my own, apart from and mostly at odds with my family. The friendly beings departed or faded away when I went to school. Mother had already increased her alcohol intake when she moved to California. She continued to drink more often and to increase her intake throughout my childhood.

It has taken years to see and accept the longer-lasting effects of living with an alcoholic/gone mother that tend to show up in my relationships: my fear of abandonment, anxiety about doing the right thing, being the right person. To this day, I often lack focus and determination to take care of my own life and needs, follow my own creative urges. I allow other peoples' lives and priorities to overshadow mine. I have difficulty making decisions, simply declaring what I want and what I don't want. My father mostly was not with us, and when he was, paid little or no attention to me at all. As a result, I believe I often run up against my own ignorance and assumptions about men in relationships. I think fathers also help us to stand, or take a place in the world, a major unclear concept about life to me.

As a young adult with a child, I moved back to California in 1974. I had not seen my dad since 1960, when my family had moved to Virginia. Dad would sometimes come to visit me in San Francisco, especially after I had divorced my husband and was dating J, an architect. Dad, who had not finished his degree in architecture, was nevertheless a talented builder. He admired J and wanted to do something for him. J had loaned me his prized 1964 Chevy pick-up to do some hauling and Dad decided to give the truck a tune up. By the time J came to bring his truck home, the engine was a pile of parts. J had to hire a guy to finish the job. Dad was apologetic, but disappeared quickly after that.

He reappeared a month later with a new wife, an infantile and sappy woman from Clear Lake. They were on their way north to honeymoon near Clear Lake. The marriage lasted about one month and Dad was back again at my door, needing a place to stay for the night. He suggested we sleep together so we could get to know each other better. If that didn't work for me, perhaps he could sleep with my five year old daughter. Fathers and grandfathers know best how to instruct their children in the ways of sex and relationships, he believed. I fixed him a bed on my living room floor and told him if I heard anymore creepy stuff like that, he would have to go. He left the next day.

He didn't visit often after that, and I did not call him or "court" him in any way. I had at one time thought I could finally, as an adult, have a relationship with my dad. But I had also come to see how sick he was inside, how little influence I would have over his weird thoughts and behaviors, and how little of me he was truly interested to know. Years passed. One day I felt compelled to visit my grandmother in the desert. I thought that maybe she was dying, and I had better go. So I packed up my camper, and loaded up my fifteen-year old daughter and three-year old son and drove to Yucca Valley.

Grandma Jen was as effusive and sweet as ever. Only one problem: she had developed a form of dementia that prevented her from making any sense with words—but the loving tone and inflection were still there. Dad was living there, too. As evening descended, Grandma Jen sat down to her Hammond organ to play something for me. The music was exactly like her speech—notes, chords and rhythms were all there but none of it made sense. I started to cry and decided to slip out a side door so she would not see. From another room in the house, Dad slipped out into this same transition zone between Jen's house and the neighbors, and walked toward me. When we were face to face, he looked directly into my eyes and expressed his great sorrow that he had not been a better father to us kids, and especially to me. He was aware that he had nearly missed me as a child and that his life had been chaotic and unhealthy, no fit state for getting to know children.

I was forty years old, and for about two minutes I finally had an open, loving relationship with my dad. These moments, so few, were over like *that*! Gone. Never to return. Dad was quickly back to his delusional self. But for those two minutes I had him all to myself, and there was clarity and caring between us. And forgiveness. It was a small miracle that I have never forgotten, nor ever will. Reflecting on this event later, I realized that it was Dad I had come to see. Grandma Jen was in some way already "gone" and did not appear to gain anything from my visit. But those few magical moments with my dad made all the difference in my life, and maybe in his, too. I'll never know.

I'm still growing, still learning, still opening to the present me, albeit influenced by my past but living and loving now in spite of it. I maintain a spiritual practice that includes meditation. I am learning *Focusing*, a consciousness practice that allows me to listen inside and approach with friendliness, the embodied feeling-sense of my experiences and emotional triggers. Combining meditation and Focusing helps me to create some "right distance" from the hard stuff of life, and make distinctions about my embodied traumas. Attending Al-Anon provides me with a frequent opportunity to make "confession" about the many little failures and dilemmas in my life and relationships, to be visible and vulnerable with a group of people who know what I am talking about, and to be of service to the recovering community. This life of mine is a work-in-progress.

Prologue

"ABANDON ALL HOPE, YE WHO ENTER HERE." Hope is a wonderful quality to possess, a fortifying state of being to call forth. But in certain situations, hope is not a useful state in which to dwell, and utterly useless in the trenches with alcoholics. If you are a child of alcoholic parents, hope can become a weapon of self-destruction in your daily life. In co-dependent children hope can become concretized, attached to specific outcomes and ways of achieving them. Hope diverts attention from the truth of the predicament, and sends serenity on negative missions through an inner maze of motivations, agendas and expectations. With an alcoholic you need to don your self-preservation helmet and, perhaps, prick up your best warrior instincts.

With Em I never gave up on her soul, on her goodness, brightness, generosity or the possibility of sobriety. Not giving up was a more powerful stance for me than to hope she would stop drinking. Not giving up was something I could do.

Gone to Grace Land (2014)

Emily died. She took another human with her that day. We can argue the facts 'til the cows come home; we can certainly have pity on the family whose son was unexpectedly swooped up that day. I will never be able to think of Emily without remembering her suffering, her pain, her laugh, her shining presence, and her gone-to-hell other side. Now I can see how shaky was her hold on life, and how valiant her efforts to stay with us, despite knowing that she might have died a thousand times before in a thousand similar circumstances, before this final time.

Emily was my sister's oldest daughter, the one I passed the family ring to 14 years after I received it. Emily remained my always funny and loving niece though many years might fly by in both our lives, with little contact between us. In 1986 my youngest son was born and Em was working for a chic clothing producer and living in San Francisco. The day Emily came to visit and take care of me and baby Jules, she became my friend. Family obligation may have brought her to my house that day, but her kindness and service to my mental and physical health, and the soulful conversations we initiated shifted our relationship to one that became a source of strength for me, lasting her lifetime and beyond.

There were long lapses in communication for a few years after those times in 1986, but every connection we made enriched me. Her letters, cards and poetry inspired me to write more, share more and shed more caution. The more we talked or wrote, emailed and texted, sharing more intimate and searching thoughts and beliefs, the closer we became. At times, I was teacher; at times, it was Emily teaching, groping for meaning or logic in her troubled life and bringing her findings to the table. At times I played historian for the gaps in her family knowledge, and she filled in her personal history gaps for me.

Her stories opened a space in me to hold and grow compassion for my sister who had always been tough karma for me, and certainly was for Emily, too. Emily never blamed her parents for her own dysfunctions and addictions; she held for their greatest fault being only their denial—she felt especially wounded by her mother's seeming inability to accept her and believe her story, Emily's own account of her childhood. It doesn't matter what the facts are, we all have to work with the *perceptions* we form and embody from when we absorbed impressions through our skin.

Stories. We told our stories: what our experiences appeared to have been, and how it now appeared to us, as a way of tracking our progress. We whooped in celebration—"wee doggie!"—cried in mock pain—"whaaaa." Sometimes we just cried—in joy or in sorrow or confusion. When I told Em that one of my favorite teachers said all stories are psycho-diagnostic, we laughed together heartily and knowingly until our bellies ached. We shared esoteric knowledge—shamanic healing, meditation, consciousness, and books. We stayed on each other's prayer and gratitude lists. We sometimes did energy work together. And sometimes I spoke to the ancestors for Emily, recruiting their help on her behalf, and on behalf of generations to come.

For a couple of years, my cell phone stayed on my nightstand. If Emily called in the middle of the night, and she sometimes did, I could talk her off the ledge of her nightmares. I wasn't freaked out about her panic attacks, because I saw these terrifying episodes first as a spiritual issue that precipitated physical reactions, not the reverse. I became a lightning rod until she could find her body again. In those last few years of her life, she reported that the episodes came less frequently and were less intense, almost manageable.

She confessed to drinking caffeinated beverages to get high, drinking beer to come down. She also let me know that she was not always sober when purported to be. I was grateful, if saddened, by her admissions. Our celebrations of her year or more of sobriety were not exactly kosher AA, and perhaps desperate attempts to feel better about herself.

Em seemed to have gotten all the live genetic markers for alcoholism from both sides of her family. She was profoundly addicted most of her life. She had been in and out of rehab and detox centers many,

many times over the years. Her own father told me: "I've never met anyone who tried so hard to stay sober." And he should know, having been in AA for over 40 years.

Years ago, when I realized how addicted she was and how out of control she could be, when Em's daughter went to live with her grandmother (my sister), I decided privately to never give up on her, just as I had privately decided to never give up on my alcoholic mother. Because there was so much confusion, grief and contention in our family, I did not always speak up about my resolution. As Em and I got to know each other better, I told her that I had and would always believe in her, hold her in love and faith, always pray for her safety, happiness and health.

Her last few years were a bit more generally sober. The nightmarish panic attacks came about every 6 months and lasted a few minutes or a day. Regardless, Em had married a beautiful man and re-united with her daughter, Lauren, and they had a lot of good time together. Em and her younger sister, Marjorie, were re-united after 20 years of estrangement. They spent the holidays together, and pulled off a major hiking-camping trip with Marj's three kids and husband, and Em's husband and the dogs. The last time Em and her husband came to visit my brother and me and our kids, we got together in my brother's family restaurant, just like old times.

Now I want to tell you about the night Emily died. She had called me early in the day of April 25, 2013, three weeks after her 49th birthday. I had turned off the volume on my phone to focus on some business writing. I listened to her message on my way out to see some clients at 4 pm. She was on her way to Palmdale that morning and as the drive was long and boring maybe I could call her back. "Just checking in.... love you!"

I went to work thinking I would call her later. After work I was going to attend my first class in shamanic healing. Since Emily was involved in the Shamanic Healing Center in L.A., and loved the work, I couldn't wait to "report" on my first experience.

Our teacher, Korie, led us on a few practice journeys to get used to the protocols, the drumming, and to get introduced to our power animal guide. On the last journey, our task was to ask our power animal what we needed to know for that journey. I met my guide, a female panther, who came to escort me down into the lower world.

I asked my power animal if there was something I needed to know at this time. She looked at me with her great green eyes, daring me to follow, and took off. I jumped onto her back and we fled somewhere deep into that world. At one point I stopped trying to see where we were going and dropped onto her back, my arms and hands reaching down into her paws. I seemed to merge with her. We scampered as one.

"We must gather up the lost souls and some old ones," I heard her say in my mind. Upon hearing that thought I noticed a clearing bathed in gold light. My panther friend, paced just outside the circle of light and I knew she was containing the lost souls within that fire-like light. Off to the right I sensed, rather than saw, a group of 'old ones' waiting. I was simply to know this, but not interfere.

After sharing my journey with the group, the only feedback I remember receiving was that I was there to witness something, and in future journeys I might go back and ask my power animal for more information. We closed the circle, and I went out into the night for a short walk. The weather was very fine and slightly warm. I felt happy, and a little excited, without really knowing why. After a short walk around town, I started back up the hill outside the studio where we had journeyed that evening. A large white owl crossed overhead, just in front of me and landed on the building next to the studio. Wow! It had been, and continued to be, a magical night.

As I walked on toward my car, I remembered Emily's call. Maybe I can call her tonight, maybe it won't be too late, I'll be home in a couple of minutes...

I opened my front door at 10 pm. I thought, "Damn. I should have called her right after class. It's too late...I'll call her in the morning."

At 9 am next morning my sister called with the news that Emily had died last night at 9:49 pm. At the same time the owl flew over my head.

In a state of shock and overwhelming grief, I forgot all about the content of the journey, only that something had happened and I wanted to tell her about it. I had missed my opportunity.

Several weeks later I remembered the journey. I reviewed the scant notes I had taken in class and consulted with my teacher, Korie. She confirmed that I must have been called to witness Em's passing. The old ones were waiting to carry her on to her new level. Korie said, "Sometimes death *is* the healing."

I went home and planted sunflowers for Emily.

During my period of grieving my ancestor altar took a journey of its own, dis-assembled and moved around to different rooms, and then resettled again in the place it had started. Emily's picture now sits beside photos of my mother and her great grandmother Florence, overlooked by *my* great grandmother, also a Florence.

Emily appeared in dreams and in journeys in the first year after her passing. In one dream, my long-deceased Mother drives me to a location where there is a small apartment. She stays in the car as I go in. I have an encounter with the Egyptian demi-god, Anubis. I look out the window to the left and see that Mother has gone, and out the window on the right and see two women lying in the yard of a corner house across the street. One is not moving, and I know it is Emily. Then, we are down on the bank of a river, and Anubis is there again. Emily stands with eyes closed.

When I woke from this dream, I went immediately to one of my books, written by a friend who links the Egyptian pantheon of gods with modern western astrological planets and deities. Sure enough, there was a picture of Anubis, just as I had seen him in the dream. He's the one sporting a jackal's head. Had you asked me to identify any Egyptian gods before this dream, I could not have done it. But in the dream I knew it was Anubis. According to the author, he is connected to the under/other world, and helps souls *cross over*. In modern western astrology, Anubis is associated with Chiron, the Wounded Healer archetype. Em and I know Chiron well.

In classical Tarot, Anubis is associated with the Hanged Man. Like the Hanged Man, his perspective is reversed. He dangles from the World Tree held by the Serpent of Life. He is poised over the River Nile awaiting return to his father, Osiris.

From *Shamanic Mysteries of Egypt* by Linda Star-Wolf:

> In order to take on an entirely fresh perspective, you have to sacrifice or let die your old way of being, including your old way of seeing. Every time that a human goes upward into spirit or a god goes downward into human form, there is either an expansion or a contraction of consciousness. When gods become human they have to contract enough to forget some of their divinity in order descend into matter.

I like to think of Emily, and all my departed friends and relations, as having gone into an expanded state of consciousness, no longer a particle in form, but a wave of light. In fact, my mother came to visit shortly after she died. I was in that liminal state before waking, where I became aware of morning, but was not yet fully awake. I can still see her face, so beautiful, loving and wise. "I've come to tell you I'm in a new *light*." I was so startled to see her, and so happy, she repeated: "It's okay, honey. I just came to tell you I'm in a new light." She always said if she could, she would, come back and tell me all about it. She left me with a sweet mystery to ponder the rest of my days.

From *Shamanic Egyptian Astrology* by Star-Wolf and Ruby Falconer:

> It is Anubis who helps each of us through the transition time between the worlds, and most of all, it is he who opens us, renews us, and washes away the pain and suffering of our old incarnation so that we may once again be made whole. His role as a *renewer of life*—not just a guardian of the dead—cannot be overemphasized. (Italics mine)

Three weeks ago was Emily's birthday. She would have been 50, her "Chiron return" as the astrologers say. At Korie's shamanic journey circle I asked my friends to see if any messages are waiting for me in the other world. It has been a year, tomorrow, since Emily left, and I am probing the edges of my sensitivity to be aware of rising grief, or any work yet to be done. Many wonderful insights came to me that night, and a few practical suggestions, which I have heartily undertaken.

Our circle also welcomed a new woman that night. Without knowing anything about Emily or the circumstances of her death or even my first journey the night she died, this new woman had a powerful experience of Emily. Nicole came back from our first journey with an overwhelming sense of a radiating love seen and felt from Em to me and to our family. She choked up a little just remembering the clarity and intensity of the love and light. She paused a moment. Then she looked at me and asked, "Does the prayer of St. Francis mean anything? I kept hearing bits of it…" Then love overtook me, and I cried, for wonder, joy and mystery. Later Nicole came to my house and I showed her the book marker, made by one of Emily's friends for her memorial, with Em's picture and her favorite prayer,

the **Prayer of Saint Francis of Assisi:**

Lord, make me an instrument of thy peace;

where there is hatred, let me sow love;

where there is injury, pardon;

where there is doubt, faith;

where there is despair, hope;

where there is darkness, light;

where there is sadness, joy

O divine master,

grant that I may not so much seek to be consoled as to console;

to be understood, as to understand;

to be loved, as to love.

For it is in giving that we receive,

it is in pardoning that we are pardoned,

and it is in dying that we are born to Eternal Life.

Amen

At the bottom of the bookmark is a quote from Pema Chodron, who has written a brilliant book, *When Things Fall Apart*—"Nothing ever goes away until it has taught us what we need to know."

Thanks, Em. I am here to learn. My guilt, sorrow, grief, regret and emptiness are rapidly transforming into grace. I look forward to my journey circle tonight, to all our journeys, as they show the tendency of our lives to reveal the beauty, logic and mystery of the universe we live in, if we simply look.

Note: Originally, my account of Emily's passing included the deaths of two other friends—Emily died on Erica's birthday; Erica succumbed to cancer a month after Emily died; Billy Joe died of cancer two weeks after Erica. After Billy Joe passed, the haunting first journey experience with "the lost souls and the old ones" lifted, and I knew my witnessing role for this time was complete.

PART I:

Truth and Lie

CHAPTER 1: Drunk and Disorderly

"I was violating my standards faster than I could lower them," quipped Robin Williams, describing in characteristic and somewhat caustic manner, the speed with which he lost control and all anchoring in sobriety after 20 years of avoiding alcohol and all other substances.

MOST DRUNKS DO NOT KILL THEMSELVES and their families in spectacular car wrecks on the way home from a party. More likely, drunks kill the **spirit** of their families, especially the children, slowly and predictably enslaving them in shame, rage, denial and a warped sense of self. As they say in AA: "Hurt people hurt people."

Alcohol, it is said, lifts inhibitions. Whatever aspect hides inside, with alcohol, comes out to play with whoever is at hand. Some drunks exhibit a rise in sullen, resentful anger, some explode in violence; some become joyful and sweet, while others go for the numbing effect, or they turn inward to attend to private fantasies, and with more alcohol, they sail beyond numb to nothing, no thought, no feeling, blackout.

When the veil that inhibited her deeper unconscious memories and tendencies was lifted or washed away with spirits, my mother became more talkative, happy and lovingly available. Mother drank to dispel fear and to feel good about herself, to forget her anxiety about life and people, money and responsibilities. A few drinks to take the edge off; a few more to encourage her inner child—magical, innocent and wounded—to emerge. A few more and the universal loving acceptance degrades to sloppy sentiment. A few more and the Wounded Child's shame becomes histrionic recap of sad life events. Eventually, a depressing moroseness shows up to mourn her loss of innocence. Down near the end of the bottle, blessed numbness.

My brother, sister and I were the stranded, bereft witnesses.

Alcoholism was an ongoing, daily issue in my family, though we rarely, if ever, talked openly about it. Alcohol was another member of our family, given a special place at the table, special considerations. Always on the shopping list, though never written down. Alcohol intruded upon and controlled every family gathering like a rude uncle or a disliked but necessary in-law.

The following memories are mostly from age nearly 10 to nearly 20, told my way, as I remember them. I did not consult anyone in the writing of these memories and will do nothing to alter them, except perhaps to change the names of those involved. If anything, they are glimpses into my family, glimpses of life with an alcoholic mother and absent father. They serve to illustrate some traits or qualities commonly found in people who drink or use drugs excessively and compulsively.

MEMORIES: Across the street from my childhood

My brother always wants to go back. He has to visit our childhood home whenever he goes to L.A. Sometimes we all go—Brent and his wife and daughter; my sister and her husband, and me with or without husband. A few months before Mother died, we took her, too. Sometimes my sister's daughters go. Once I took my daughter; once I went alone. Sometimes no one wants to go with Brent, so he slips out in the morning with a cup of coffee while the rest of us are getting showered and organized for the day. He drives around Redondo Beach: the pier, Riviera Village, Nardone's, and Millie Riera's Seafood Grotto—the restaurant lounge where our mother had her own stool at the bar—and the esplanade, the concrete walkway stretching from Redondo to Marina Del Rey and beyond.

He often drives up to our old neighborhood, an area the developers named "Hollywood Riviera" in an attempt to entice the Hollywood stars to buy homes at the beach. But the stars wanted to shine on Rodeo drive, so it became a working-class community for everyone but the most famous. Our dad was lured away from the University of Virginia by the promise of wealth in the California post-war building boom. He and mom were "that close" to finishing their degrees in architecture and engineering. They never did. Instead, Dad built our home in Hollywood Riviera, then sent for Mother, my older sister and baby Brent.

"I went up to the house," Brent says after one of his treks to the old homestead, his strong, clear voice softer now and hushed. Eyes shining with reverence in his private joy, he might be saying, "I went up to Taj Mahal." This ritual defines my brother in his element.

He reports on his findings—there's a garden now in the front, and, they changed the garage around so the door faces the street, or, there are roses in front... His first report came about eight years after our family moved east. Brent had joined the Naval Air Reserve and was stationed for a time in San Pedro. My sister had moved back to California the year before, away from Virginia and back to Redondo as quickly as possible. Brent often spent weekends with my sister and her kids.

"They took down Mother's avocado tree." This first report was the saddest of all. Mother loved that avocado tree into producing fruit just to spite our gardener who said it wouldn't. Mother sprouted, then planted, the seed of the first avocado consumed in our house. The tree grew well for several years, but stopped. The gardener said it would never survive, or if it did, never bear fruit.

Sometime later, we had a noteworthy earthquake—unlike the

frequent little tremors too commonplace to mention. In the next three years the avocado grew ten feet, above the roof edge. Mother reasoned the tree's roots had been stopped by the concrete foundation, which the earthquake damaged just enough to allow the roots to roam free and the tree to grow again. Like the tree, my mother had persistently pursued life through monumental forces and unnatural impediments. The tree rewarded her care and faithfulness with abundant fruit the year before we left.

"I went up to the house—they let me in to look around," Brent offers in his quiet excitement after one such visit. He pauses, gauging my facial contortions. "The fruit trees in the back are gone, so are Mother's roses. But it looks real nice inside."

I am torn. His childhood was evidently more joyful and memorable to him than mine was to me. And, I realize he has become one of the most sentimental, emotional men I have ever known.

One visit to L.A., Brent, my sister and I made the trek up to our old house. I sat on a curb across the street from my childhood and watched my brother and sister walk up and down reliving theirs.

I needed a small distance between the house and me. I let my imagination go for me, up the drive and the steps as I remembered them, into the past and gone. I can't face the front in my mind, so I float 'round to the side yard and my first garden. Before I can fully picture my little carrots picked too soon, the snails and worms and flowers, the vision swirls into a dusty vagueness. Around again to the backyard and a fig tree growing up through the hole in a round wooden table where Mother sits with a cup of coffee, dreamily slurping juicy figs, smiling in the morning sun. A tiny pair of gritty hands pushes a fresh mud pie up toward her smile. "Oh, honey, how wonderful," she beams and pretend-plucks a few bites to go with her fig.

Dust swirls the images away again. I glance up the ice plant covered embankment behind the house. Up to the backyards above, to a girl on a swing, braces on her legs. I cannot remember her name.

My brother and sister study the front yard, the garage, the fences and trees. I am glad they are wrapped around each other and their discoveries. My face is wet and I need distance from them, too. It was not back then, or ever, safe for me to display emotion in front of them. I spent a great deal of my childhood feeling choked up about something or other, and quickly learned to hold in or face criticism from my brother that was about equal to having my feelings lampooned or rationalized away by my sister. The two together was too much.

I am swirled away again, into the house, into the kitchen. Mother at the kitchen sink on her day off, staring out the window, humming or singing to herself. It seems to take all day for her to do the dishes. Sometimes she cooks, but mostly she putters in that small zone—table to stove to sink to refrigerator to counter to table...

Sad music fills the house. Brent and sister, Dee, have made their escapes early in the day. I am alone with her in the house—more alone with her here than when she is gone. She mutters and hums, putters with dishes, looks out the window, hums and whistles. The water swooshes on with a high whine through the Faucet Queen sprayer, clunks off again, jolting the pipes somewhere under the sink. Throughout the dull afternoon: *shweee*—on, *kunk*—off. Sometimes in the night I hear the water, *shweee*—*kunk*. An hour or a few minutes later: *shweee*—*kunk*. Later still, *shweee*—*kunk*.

She pours vodka to the half way mark made by her middle finger around a Tom and Jerry cartoon jelly glass then tops it with water—*shweee-kunk*. Moody Mozart, sweet Brahms, or tragic operas lengthen the afternoon. *Shweee-kunk*. The house sags around me and

I retreat to my bed and cry myself to sleep in the middle of a sunny day, with the whine and clunk from the far away kitchen, a foghorn sounding across a dark ocean, rocking me a-raft at sea.

I could play near her, in the playroom she created out of our dining room. But often the music is just too loud. And to hear her mumble and hum, or da-dee-dah-dum the piano concertos sets off strange feelings in me—a fear that took years to identify: My mother isn't there. She has gone away, out the kitchen window, up the cinder block wall and ice plant embankment and beyond. Her body in the kitchen frightens and saddens me.

A cloud of vague sights and sounds gather around me on the curb. Brent and Dee chat and laugh as they wander down the block a few yards toward Candy's old house. They look back at me to shout some part of the story they are telling each other—their voices barely cover the distance. They laugh, so I smile and wave, and they move on, their voices fade again. Dust is dry in my throat.

There is always a residue of sadness, incompleteness, loss and pain within me. Longing is the ambient noise of my experience, the tune playing just below the range of my hearing and deciphering. I am seventy years old and I cannot remember when these feelings were not present. They live and replicate in my very cells. Opera still makes me cry—partly for its beauty and purity, partly for my memories of it blaring through the house, captivating my mother and carrying her away. All children of alcoholics I have ever known were terribly lonely kids, trapped by their own need for their alcoholic parents, their needs for soothing and the simple recognition of attention.

Elie Wiesel said,
**"An abnormal response to an abnormal situation
is normal."**

In 1960 Mother sold our house and bought a travel trailer. We embarked on a road trip across the U.S. that was, I believe, my mother's one chance to do something grand, her one opportunity to tour national parks and the wonders of this country, to deeply enjoy the outdoors, to educate her kids in geology, history, biology, the mix of cultures and the ever-changing plant life across America, and to create lasting memories for us all. Our original intention was to take the summer to ramble eastward, seeing the sights. We just kept going, following interesting roads, taking our time.

Mostly, Mother drank less while we traveled. At times, when she drank she was child-like, friendly and generous with other people—she held naive assumptions about everyone's basic grace and goodness—and put us at risk with every drink.

The morning after a blow-out party in our near-empty house, we piled into the car, with trailer attached and began our odyssey toward our new home in Virginia. I was nearly 10; my sister, Dee, was 14; brother Brent, 12. We tooled around California, visited "Uncle" Hill and his two kids in Berkeley and went to the San Francisco Zoo. I thought I would freeze to death there by the beach. It was foggy (what else?) and our summer clothes were no match for the cold. I was allowed to buy a sweat shirt. But I didn't get to wear it. I had been begging my mother and sister to take me to a bathroom, I was desperate to pee. They were so busy talking with other people—Mother and Hill, Dee and our cousins—that they did not pay any attention, though I asked several times. My sister finally sneered at me, "It's over *there!*" But I could not see a sign anywhere, so I sat down on a curb, out of the fray of people moving and talking over me, and peed. When I was done I tied the sweatshirt around my waist to cover my wet bottom, and ran to catch up to the family herd already moving on without me.

This little embarrassing vignette seemed to typify my plight among family—at crucial moments I can't get a word in edgewise, no one seems to notice or care that I am in distress, whatever I need comes in dead last. That day in the zoo I cried through about half of it, feeling miserable and cold and both baffled by and infuriated by my family. My brother and sister seemed to have a grasp on the world that I did not, possessing a kind of assurance about themselves that I did not; they seemed to know who they were and their place in the world. I did not. I had become the victim and scapegoat, a burden, and could see no further than that.

One of our last stops in California before leaving the state was to visit my father in Ukiah. He had a girlfriend there who lived in a nice house with a small pool. Dad met us in a parking lot to pick up Brent. Mother and Dee had made plans to visit the Italian Swiss Colony Winery (how appropriate). No one had asked me, they just assumed I would go with Mother and Dee. But something in me began to long desperately to be with my dad, as if I might never see him again, and this was my last chance. I whimpered to my mother that I wanted to go with him and Brent. Everyone seemed shocked at the request. Dad was kind about it, and actually apologized that he, like everyone, thought I would want to go with Mother. He welcomed me into his plan with Brent. Whenever he visited us, he had never much taken notice of me, so it was a big deal to get to go with him.

He took us to McDonald's for burgers (my first time) and then to his girlfriend's house. We changed into our suits and jumped into the pool. Pretty soon it was apparent to me that Dad and Brent were an item, swimming to the deep end of the pool and having private fun activities. Once again, I was left to myself. I remember creeping on tip toe to the edge of the deep end, having to lift my chin out of the water, barely able to keep from going under. I wondered if I did go under, would they even notice? I don't remember that Dad even spoke to me again after we got in the pool. He seemed remote as ever, unattainable, impervious to my need of him. By nearly ten, I was accustomed to holding in for fear of judgmental reactions from my brother and sister. I was trained to be nice, be quiet and not make waves, and to not appear to need anything. And by all means, to not call attention to myself.

By early July we had been touring American Indian ruins and canyons of the Southwest and had parked our travel trailer in Flagstaff to facilitate day trips to the Grand Canyon, Wupatki ruins, and other assorted sights. I remember the stifling 120 degree heat of Bryce Canyon, made worse by the uniformity of color—pink—everywhere, every rock, the canyon walls, the air itself—close, hot and dusty pink. I stumbled along behind my small family, sleep walking in the heat. Suddenly, my head turned to the left, I stepped off to the left and walked about ten feet away from the trail. I looked down to millions of dusty pink rocks and without thinking, picked one up.

It was caked with pink dust, which when removed, showed the rock to be a 2-inch long cylinder. I could see one end was wider than the other and had the impression that it may be hollow, and I could see the *inside* of the rock was caked with dust. I dug it out, shook it out, knocked out the dirt to find a cylinder of pink rock with an interior lining of clear crystal! What an amazing find. My brother was impressed for five seconds. My mother came over to look and we engaged around the origins of this rock, and how it may have formed from a volcano, and so forth. Brent walked on, clucking his tongue; Dee derided and judged, heaping stupid all over my precious find and mother's interest in it. And, "can't we get out of here? It's too hot to stand here with you two going on and on about a stupid rock!"

Mother, of course, complied and we moved on. I knew my mother was genuinely interested but would act aloof for the sake of peace. Because I had found this awesome treasure, my brother and sister disdained it, looked down their collective noses at it, and at me for my intrigue with it. Alone, isolated and no one to share my treasure with. The most amazing part of this story to me is that this rock *called* to me—that's the only way I can say it. Pulled me to itself. I was in a stupor from the heat and the monotonous dusty pinkness of the canyon, the trail, everything. But something made me turn left, walk over, bend down and deliberately pick up this particular rock, out of all the other dusty pink bits on the ground. It's a mystery I have shared with a few friends and enjoyed thinking about all my life, 60 plus years so far, and will continue to appreciate until I die and beyond. In all my misery and isolation, *something* had given me a gift, a treasure, and I felt special, singled out in a good way. It was not safe to share this private joy with my family, so I kept it to myself.

Today, this lovely treasure sits on my ancestor altar, and has served as a link between me and the other realms, a listening tool in the quest for spiritual guidance. The conflict within me was feeling as if the Universe has singled me out, I have a special purpose that no one, not even me, knows about, in strong contrast to deep isolation and loneliness, of belonging nowhere and having no particular reason to be. This conflict is still with me today, though perhaps less intensely felt and less powerfully influential.

Rather than drive back to the trailer after a day in 120-degree heat on the floor of Bryce Canyon, we took cheap air-conditioned motel rooms. Brent wanted his own space and was granted a room one adjoining door away from where I would sleep between my sister and my mother, when she got back from the bar, that is.

We three kids bedded down in our respective rooms while Mother went out to explore the local fauna at the truck-stop watering hole adjacent the motel. She made instant friends over a few drinks and would have trusted any of them with her life. Or ours. One newly found buddy was a long way from home. Mother, ever the friend to another drinker, offered the man to share Brent's room for the night.

A short time later, Brent burst into our room, wide-eyed and white-faced in terror. He had awakened to a strange, smelly man groping his groin and offering an exchange of favors.

"Aw, now, Bren," Mother cooed, "he's a nice guy, he just needed a place to sleep." Brent raged. Mother would not entertain the notion that my brother had been in danger, let alone that his personhood and sense of safety had been violated. My sister and I rolled over and went back to sleep. I was disturbed but at the time did not understand his terror and anger. Mother never acknowledged his rage and pain. He never trusted her again.

When Mother was drinking, everyone was her friend, trustworthy, sweet. There seemed to be no room in her for entertaining another option—sociopath? serial killer? loser? Drunk, she was indiscriminate, incautious, oblique. This dangerous form of denial put my brother at risk, and she was incapable of seeing the violation, or even hearing about his experience.

After wandering a bit in the Southwest, we meandered back up through Nevada, Idaho, Wyoming and into Montana, skipping the Dakotas. In Idaho, Mother followed her nose down a country road, heading vaguely north. It was beautiful, rolling farmland—a great relief from the heat of the desert. After a while I noticed a dead sheep just inside a pasture fence. Then another. We began to drive more slowly and peer beyond the fences to see other dead animals—a horse, birds, other sheep. We passed houses but never saw a human being. It was spooky. After an hour or so, Mother decided to get out of there and turned the car around rather than to drive through this macabre scene any longer. We never had an explanation for what we saw, nor for what we did not see: people. I have since wondered if there was perhaps a toxic gas leak somewhere, or an experiment with animals that went wrong. We were never able to find out what happened in this farming community. By the time we found a small town, no one there could tell us anything either.

On to Montana and Teton Lake! Our first viewing of a moose in the wild. Our dog, Rover, wanted very badly to go after this gentle creature for some reason. But the moose was up to over his knees in the lake, placidly chomping green stuff and our dog was a little guy who couldn't swim and be fierce at the same time. He reluctantly gave up chase. That night we watched the aurora borealis play across the skies over the Grand Tetons.

We traveled back south to the Texas coast, where my brother and I dropped lines in the bay at Corpus Christi and amazed the locals by how many fish we landed in a very short period of time. We gave them all away. From there, we headed East to New Orleans. I had my tenth birthday at Court of Two Sisters, a rather elegant and old, famous restaurant. My daughter, who now lives nearby, says that restaurant still stands, and is still considered one of the best. After New Orleans, our course took us through the South, where we still had family: Alabama, Florida and North Carolina.

We arrived in Asheville, North Carolina well after dark but Mother was determined to find her way up the winding road to Unc's house on Beaucatcher Drive. She had been drinking since entering her home state and as we neared our destination the gloom of her life and memories closed in. Years later I would learn we were on the same road where 15 years earlier, when Mother was very pregnant with Dee, my father had opened the door on her side of their old Merc, right where a steep embankment dropped away from the road, and violently tried to push her out, his *first* attempt to kill her.

My sister argued and pleaded with Mother to stop safely, stop weaving, stop telling stupid stories, get coffee, let *me* drive…I woke when my sister became nearly hysterical with rage, fearing that Mother would steer the car, with travel trailer in tow, off that road's shear drop, where it would roll down into the woods and we would all die in a ball of flames.

"Oh, now, Deesy…" Mother slurred as she rifled her purse for a cigarette. "We'll be there any minute." Mother turned in her seat and winked at me in the backseat, un-lit cigarette dangling from her mouth. Eyes still on me, not on the road ahead, Mother slapped her hand around the dashboard to find the cigarette lighter. She hit the headlights instead. We were in total darkness and still weaving on the road.

Dee screamed, "Stop the car. Now!" Finally, Mother complied and Dee and I climbed into the trailer to await our doom. Dee was determined not to die in the car with Mother, but preferred to perish in our own spectacular propane fireball, thank you very much. Brent, sleeping soundly in the back seat of the car, would never know what hit him.

Somehow we made it to Unc's that night. I don't remember much after Dee and I got into the trailer. But I do remember denying, doubting, then partly waking up to, the danger we were in with Mother drunk and beyond all sense and logic, weaving all over the small, winding, utterly dark road. I remember feeling anxiously divided between Dee's rational rage and Mother, alone behind the wheel. Not that I could have controlled the car, but felt I might have been able to keep her awake.

Awakening to the danger we could be in also awakened me to the terrible, stressful conflict I felt, divided between my mother's bleary-eyed smile and my sister's rage and fear. Who knew better? Mother had driven across the country without a scratch, except for a few holes in the trailer caused by the fins on the car, and Dee had bitched and moaned about almost everything for thousands of miles. She was genuinely frightened, however, and crying, desperate, angry and feeling helpless. Looking back, I think this night of terror on the road traumatized my sister and broke whatever bond of love and loyalty she had with our mother, and possibly our family. Less than two years later she would leave to marry and start her own family. I think she couldn't wait to get away from all of us.

We lived in that 20' x 8' travel trailer—Mother, 3 kids and a small dog—for another year after reaching Virginia, late in 1960. My bed alternated between the small berth I shared with my mother or the other one I might share with my sister; Brent slept in the fold-down bed at the front of the trailer with our dog, Rover, in the small drawer at the end of his bed. We joked about becoming trailer trash.

Unc and Margery came up from Asheville to visit during our first Christmas. We partied at Aunt Emily's house in Arlington—dinner and drinks and stories from their childhood. We three kids and our two cousins exhausted all our social skills by 9 pm. Cousins went to their rooms and we three were left to wait, and wait and wait, until the adults had had all they could drink.

After many attempts to break into our elders' wandering stream of consciousness, we found places to slump and nap. Finally, we wore out our hosts and got Mother out the door and into the car. Unc and Margery followed us to our trailer for a nightcap.

Brent unfolded our small dining table, pulled the cushions together and fell into his sleeping bag. Rover, to his box. Dee had gone to a friend's house for the night. Mother and Margery sat on one bed and Unc on the other. Though dizzy from lack of sleep, there was no space for me to sit, let alone lie down. The happy adults laughed at my distress. Unc then told me they had worked it all out and I could sleep with him and Margery with Mother. Mother and Margery grinned big grins and looked at me with watery, unfocused eyes.

For a few moments I was terrified; and torn, because here was my mother's beloved brother, Unc, all the way from North Carolina, and who was I to say it was not a good arrangement. I was accommodating to all my elders—I had to be to survive in my family. I had been molested by a predator-repairman when I was 5, while my mother was gone somewhere. My habit of niceness was well established by 10.

After what seemed an eternity, the adults laughed again, and I began to breathe again after Unc explained they were all "just kidding."

"Your earliest experiences teach you who you are."

—Helen Macdonald

Scrapple Days: *During critical times in my life no one was around to guide or protect me. I couldn't get a meal some days. Peanut butter had become my staple and what little money I was given paid for school lunches and the occasional soda after school. If it weren't for my sister, we might not have eaten at all.*

By Christmas, 1961, we had a nice apartment in a fairly nice section of Arlington. Dee and Brent had their own school friends, afterschool activities, and interesting things going on in their own rooms. After all our time traveling and living in the close quarters of the trailer, I now rarely saw anyone in my family. I didn't know what to do with myself, and sought companionship with a variety of oddball kids: three giggly, dreamy girls, a 17 year-old sadly obese boy, called "Bunny," who liked to cruise the hood in his '57 Chevy, and a few real "hoods," boys destined to develop careers in drugs and crime.

I was confused when a lifeguard at the neighborhood pool paid extra attention to me. He seemed to court me, in a way, and encouraged me to flirt with him. One day he gave me a beer and a real adult passionate kiss. Of course, I thought I was in love. The next day I allowed him to lightly fondle my budding breasts through my bathing suit. Then he lectured me for 10 minutes about allowing men to take what they want. He asserted that he could have taken me "all the way" (though I did not think so) and that he and the other lifeguards had been secretly "testing" girls to see which ones were easy lays. Further, I should consider myself lucky, at 11 years old, to be out of the running for top whore around the pool. He had decided to spare me the shame of having my cherry popped by someone who did not really care about me, and warned me against further flirting. My bones rattled with rage. I felt deeply shamed, shocked to my core.

Naturally, there was no one in my family I could tell about this trap I had stepped into. The fault would have been all mine. I hope the parents of some other naïve girl busted him, or maybe that some girls' older brother would punch him out. I never went back to the pool. Years later, when I told this story to a trusted friend, she reminded me that what he had done, what many of the lifeguards were up to, would be considered statutory rape.

I turned my attention to shoplifting from the local drug store. I managed to sneak a few hair barrettes into my pocket. Next day, I picked up two candy bars and put one in my pocket. You know, *buy one, get one free.* The day after, I tried boosting a 45-rpm recording of "Earth Angel" by the Penguins and was swiftly introduced to the local police as a "potential."

Mother thought our "Uncle" Hill, who had moved to Washington just after we landed in Virginia, could be a useful male presence, keep an eye on me and maybe impose a bit of order in our home while she worked. Suddenly, an alien, uptight, militaristic, alcoholic taskmaster was in our home every afternoon—ordering us to do our homework, clean up and make dinner.

He yelled like a drill sergeant. We were terrified of Hill and furious with Mother for inviting this odious man to come down on us like a ton of bricks because she had so little control. We had met his two boys, and we liked them and felt sorry for them. We heard the demeaning way he spoke to them, the put-downs and threats, and were scandalized by his cruelty toward his own children. At least our mother did not speak to us so coldly, did not threaten violence, or abuse us to anyone who would listen to how bad we were. Dee could be critical and devilishly demanding but Hill was a devil we wanted nothing to do with.

Fortunately for us, our 'Uncle Hitler' did not last long. We rarely saw his boys and not at all after we learned that Hill's wife had run off with an office colleague, a black man (we are white), and was demanding a divorce from Hill. Within four years Hill was dead from alcoholic poisoning.

During this time, out of sheer necessity, I discovered a hidden skill to enable me to keep my small life to myself, to hide what was important. One day I came home from being out with a few friends and placed my hand on the doorknob to open the front door. I instantly froze, for I had received some inner warning feeling, an inkling about what was going on inside. I was feeling pretty happy but could not walk into the house that way. I had done that before and had my face damn near torn off because I looked and acted happy. But that day, I stretched my awareness into the apartment, to sense the home "atmosphere." I adjusted my face, my whole internal state of being, before I turned the knob, knowing in that moment just what I had to do in order to not catch some sort of hell from the tyrants on the other side of that door. It would be many years before I would realize the sort of vigilance I had developed in a family ruled by alcohol, totally lacking in guidance or protection.

Dee had maintained a relationship with a boy who lived near us in the trailer park we moved to when we first came to Virginia. Jim now came often to visit. We all liked him very much. Maybe the Uncle Hill episode pushed Dee over the rail, I don't know. I just remember it wasn't long before Dee left home to marry Jim and get pregnant. After Dee left I began to see who had really held home together and maintained a semblance of order. Quickly, stuff piled up around us. Dirty dishes haunted the limited counter spaces and sink, and rarely was food prepared for Brent and me. We had to fend for ourselves most of the time. Brent was often gone with his friends, and I was left to my own world. I could barely manage anything more complicated than heating a can of soup and making peanut butter sandwiches.

Later that year Mother ruptured a disk in her spine on her 50th birthday, by pulling a cork out of a champagne bottle. She was bed-ridden for several weeks and I had to do everything for her but get her to the toilet and back. She drank and took drugs, and slept most of the time. I know she was in great pain, but the whining and moaning drove me nuts. I felt guilty for any time I took for myself.

Though I longed to be alone, for Mother to go back to work or away, I was also lonely for a connection with her. I wanted someone to talk to, but also for friends my own age. I felt isolated and trapped most of the time.

By Christmas, 1963, Mother, Brent and I had moved to a crappy two-bedroom apartment in a dodgy part of Arlington. Brent had his own room; I shared the other room with Mother. Brent kept snakes in his room; I kept a small, clear place for myself in a cramped room crammed with clothes, boxes and too much furniture. I kept a transistor radio under my pillow. Late at night, I scanned for good music—"White Rabbit" or anything by Small Faces or other British groups. Mother worked nights, so Brent and I did not keep strict hours. The street below was alive with traffic at all hours. Brent could sleep through an A-bomb blast, but I felt unsafe there, and very much adrift, so I was often awake all hours.

Without regular cleaning our apartment was dingy and beyond cluttered. Mother had begun to collect stuff, or maybe she had too much stuff from the old, larger apartment, it was hard to tell.

She was afraid we would break some of her ancient glass Christmas ornaments. She wanted to put everything away herself. By March she got around to removing the ornaments. By then the tree had shrunk to half its former size, shed most of its needles to the floor, and disposed of two fragile figurines without any help from us.

Ornaments removed from the tree, but by no means stored safely in their boxes nor removed from the living room floor, Mother snapped and cut the tree down to a pile of stems and branches in mid-April. Every time we left the house we were expected to take a piece of the tree down to the garbage cans in the basement. I don't recall why the tree was not bagged up and brought down in one swift effort. Probably because to do so would make it obvious to the neighbors (who, we presumed, noted our every move) that our Christmas tree was still in the house four months after the time when everyone else would have disposed of theirs.

We carried the last stems out in late July. That did not mean that the precious and fragile and very old ornaments had been boxed and stored away. Oh no…

Billy, Butchie and Vernie Cleveland lived on the first floor of that roach infested apartment building; we lived directly above them. Butchie was at least twenty-seven when we met him, severely developmentally disabled and not much company to Vernie, confined to a wheelchair with MS. Billy worked outside sales for a local manufacturing company so he could be at home a lot, make meals, cleanup Vernie and Butchie, make phone calls and so forth. At night, like my mom, he drank. Vernie could put away a few, too. Butchie loved his cabbage.

One sultry summer night, televisions blaring and air conditioners humming in all units, Mother was out of alcohol. She became increasingly agitated, but had not resigned to venture out, and ABC laws in Virginia prevent stores from delivering booze. Desperate, she called Billy Cleveland. But Billy was in a similar state of dishevelment and wasn't about to run to the store or even up a flight of stairs. He was, however, working on a bottle of Jim Beam and offered Mother enough to get her to sleep.

Neither party would leave their apartment. Mother took decisive action: she looked about for a strong rope-like object to lower to Billy so he could tie on the bottle to be hoisted aloft. Lo, and behold, a 25-foot string of Xmas lights amid decorations on the floor, near the very casement window available to her and to Billy, one floor below.

Mother lowered the cord down to Billy's window. Then, deciding he should not have to work in the dark, plugged in the strand of lights—voila! Xmas in July.

I hated that old apartment. I had very little space for personal belongings and there was clutter and junk everywhere. The ironing board was seldom stowed after use and we always seemed to be walking around it to get to where we wanted to go. The dishes were nearly always piled up, and food in packages and cans were not returned to their places in the cabinets, leaving little room to prepare food. Trash overflowed the cans. We had no dining area. In fact I don't ever remember having a dining table or dining room in my youth. My mother had some old anxieties from her childhood around food and eating around other people, so we rarely ate together unless we were eating in a restaurant or at my aunt's house.

Mother's anxieties determined how we lived. That the kitchen was always in chaos and we had no place to eat, except our own laps, was connected to her stressful relationship with her bullying, alcoholic father, and how he badgered her at their dining table. It appeared as if her anxieties were the reason she drank, and they may have featured heavily in her drinking habit. But she seemed to be as addicted to her anxieties as she was to alcohol. She never got through a day without ample helpings of both.

Most alcoholics I know are like this. If they begin the day sober, there are few-to-no peaceful moments until they can drink. As the time to drink approaches, they become more agitated and anxious. Many drunks speak of not feeling normal until they can have a drink.

**He who covers up his disease
cannot expect to be cured.**

—African proverb

By age twelve, I was running away from home, first by simply staying out later and later, and then just by not coming home at all after school. Later, I ran miles away from home, and on one occasion, got a ride that took me 500 miles away, across the state line. Calling the local police to drive around the county to search for your runaway child, involves the whole machine of police and courts. I soon became a ward of the Juvenile and Domestic Relations Court of Arlington, Virginia. Having to connect cops in Arlington, with cops in Fayetteville, North Carolina involves a lot more people, a detention center, legal jurisdictions, paperwork and other stuff. I did not stop to think that by running away to another state, I was somehow sealing my fate.

I had become "incorrigible" and unruly at home and in school and had run away from home too many times. My mother could not control me—she worked odd hours and when she was home, she mostly drank and slept. My sister had gotten married and was having a kid (or vice versa) and my brother was out with his friends until all hours.

As I said, one of my run-away treks took me and two other girls across the state line and five hundred miles from home, to a small town called Fayetteville, North Carolina. My new friend, Susan, then just fourteen, "paid" our way with the driver in the front seat while my other friend, Jay, a very shy, very overweight girl of thirteen, and I sat stiffly in the back seat with the driver's buddy. I was not quite 13.

Susan disappeared our first day in town and we never saw or heard from her again. Jay and I were spotted for run-aways very soon after we hit town. We put on makeup and attempted to apply for jobs at a retail store. We thought we looked eighteen and could not understand why no one else did. Jay and I stole some food from a grocery and got separated as we ran from the grocer and his mean-looking son.

Though we had a nice place to stay—one of our new friends' mother allowed us to camp in her spare room—Jay only lasted a few days. She turned herself in to the police. Her parents were called and her angry, bullying father came to get her. I hated to think of the cruelty she would have to endure all the way back to Virginia.

I lasted a week. I lost my virginity, my dignity and what little self-esteem I might have developed before we left home. Crossing the railroad trestle one day, I heard a train coming from up the line. I looked back the way I had come and saw two police cars quickly park and four cops jump out to grab me from the other end. I would never make it back across the creek, so I made my way back just far enough that I could maybe drop from the trestle without killing myself.

I turned my body toward the tracks, dropped my feet over the side and let go. My chin hit a big beam on my way down to the beach about twelve feet below. I woke up to four laughing and shaming policemen trying to determine if I had broken my jaw. My chin bled profusely. In the end, no stitches were needed, and I came away with enough of a wound to feel I had not entirely wasted my time. After a few hours of interrogation, the cops dropped me at a safe house (detention) while my mother drove down from Virginia to bring me back.

At least with my mother, I could be cold and indifferent to her suffering, ignore her questions. I smoked cigarettes and chewed gum and said very little on the long ride back home.

Crossing a state line and having sex with "of age" boys was a big deal. Back to court (my third time) to explain to a judge what I could not then explain to myself—not only did I have no adult supervision in my life, but the adult I most depended upon was for one reason or the other not present; that I had been followed home by a drunken man who had been pressing me for weeks to "take a ride" in his car, which I had declined several times, and when I answered his knock at my door one day, he hauled off and hit me in the mouth, knocking me down and splitting my lip, because I "embarrassed" him in front of his friends; that the married, older neighbor who came to my aid that day had already tried to "get friendly" with me several times; that the boys in my school were pressing me for sex; that it wasn't safe to be a girl, had never been safe for me, ever.

The judge was getting tired of seeing me and I could offer no excuse for my behavior. The judge was tired of seeing my mother, too, and warned her that if she could not control me, I would be forced into a detention or reform school, and she would be held accountable, too. My Probation Officer was certain that I could be saved, that it would be worth it to keep me out of Detention or the notorious

Bon Aire Girls Reformatory at Lorton. On the other hand, she countered, Collier School was an institution run by Sisters of the Good Shepherd, well-educated and smart women, whose major agenda was saving "wayward girls" like me from wreck and ruin. The judge looked sternly down at me from his bench and growled, "This is your last chance!"

The summer I was thirteen, I was sent away to Collier School in New Jersey for four years, allowed a week back in Virginia once or twice per year. When we rounded the corner of the long circular driveway and pulled up in front of the girls' side of the complex, the first thing I noticed were bars on the second floor (dormitory) windows. I understood immediately: not for keeping people out; for keeping girls in!

I grew up a little in that school, learned (or remembered) that I was smart and capable, and learned to work (cleaning mostly). I was safe and safely stowed away from my family and the dangers inherent in the ending Bohemian era and the blooming Hippie age. I attended group therapy and worked with a therapist individually. I went to school and the library, worked in the girls' laundry, Sisters' kitchen, or the main house, and played basketball in the auditorium and guitar in the courtyard with other wayward girls. We had a small outdoor pool and in summer I spent as much time as I could in it. My mother had been, according to her, a "champion diver and swimmer" in her youth, so she diagrammed dives for me to practice, illustrating for me the exact form of each dive and giving me a few ideas about how to use the board, where to stand, etc.

In the dorm, each girl had a small bed and nightstand, a locker for stashing coats and books and other stuff, and occasionally we could stow a box of other personal belongings in the attic. Each of the three dorms had a large, multi-stalled, multi-sink bathroom, with showers in a common space down the hall. For three of my four years, my bed occupied a distant corner of the 28-bed St. Josephs' dorm. A radiator hummed behind my bed board, and another kept my feet warm from the wall side. Two windows, too. At night, in spite of complaints from my nearest roommate, I cracked open the window behind my bed board and listened for trains. I longed to be on a train, heading South. Away.

I did well in the sciences, English, and oddly enough, civics. I loved algebra because there were only three girls in the class and we could talk Mother Matilda into telling us stories about the other houses and girls from different eras. Matilda was at least eighty, the lenses of her glasses enlarged her eyes to twice their actual size. She was a sweetie. My biology teacher was Mother Lilian (yes, we had to call them all Mother, like I didn't have enough mother problems already). Lilian was young, probably in her early-thirties, enthusiastic to the point of leaping around the room and banging on the blackboard to make a point. She was utterly engaging.

Some of the other sisters now come to mind: Matthias who taught me to sew, and while I worked in the sisters' kitchen would come every afternoon for an onion/mayo sandwich, determined to discourage tapeworms; Roseann who could be cold and hard or dreamy and soft depending upon her rapidly shifting moods. She knew every Broadway play and helped us put on productions. Stanislas who was huge and red-faced and commanded the Sisters' kitchen with an iron will, but was really a cream puff, a giant baby; Celestine who was smart, lovely and tall, and we girls thought she looked especially beautiful when standing next to Father McNally; Bernard who was simply sweet and kind; and Pius, who had lost an arm to the giant mangle press, used to iron sheets, scapulars and hoods.

The mangle press was in the basement below the sister's chapel, and I worked there, too, for a time. It was hard to do my work on the mangle press without thinking of poor Pius, pulled by her long, belled sleeve into the hot rollers, screaming for help but not heard because no one was in the chapel at that time of day. The pain she must have endured. I couldn't wait to get out of there!

The summer before my Senior year I finally landed my ideal job: the girls' laundry. The laundry was behind the girls' kitchen, a bright and sunny room by day, and quiet but for the machines, which I did not mind. I could have a radio, but one of the girls loaned me a small record player, so I perched the player on the sill of the open window on fine days, popped Joni Mitchell on the turntable, and sang my way through washing, drying and folding. I was alone, too, which was a wonderful break from the chatter and energy of 75 girls.

Mother Brian was in charge of the girls; my mother called her the "head hood." She was tall and a bit heavy and beautiful to me. Part wild animal tamer, part mother, part psychologist, she was perfect for the job. She had a very compassionate heart and carried the right air of authority and power, which she used judiciously. She was terrifying when angry and none of us wanted to see or experience her that way. And, she could be incredibly soft and kind and insightful.

Girls sometimes ran away, walked out to the highway and hitched a ride to somewhere. One day I confessed to Mother Brian that I was desperate to get away, wanted to leave the school and not come back. I was sick of everyone. Mother Brian's response was to send me outside to work in the gardens—rake leaves, prune bushes, pick up trash, sweep the walks. I was blown away! *Outside?* Didn't you just hear me say I want to run away from this place? She heard. It was her intuitive way to give me a break and to let me know she trusted me to make a good decision. It worked brilliantly. I spent a sunny afternoon walking and puttering around the grounds, and was relieved of my distress at the end of it. Brilliant psychology.

A funny thing happened while I was a student. Vatican II. The Church made sweeping changes in the liturgy and service structure but failed to even acknowledge the needs and suggestions of the women who served her. The ranks of our sisters, as in many convents around the country, began to thin out. Lilian was first to go. By the time I graduated in 1968, Celestine and Roseann were packing to go. One year later the convent had lost every sister under age 40, and a few older ones as well.

In 1974, my first husband and I moved to San Francisco. I was in a shopping center, when I heard a nasal, Brooklyn accent calling my name: "Ayun-gie?" I knew it had to be! I turned and shouted, "Mother Brian!" She gave me that excuse-me-dear? startled and slightly offended look, then threw her finger up to her lips, and uttered a loud, "Sshhhh. It's Joan now, Joan Gillespie. But I'm married, so my new name is Joan Ray."

We visited and kept in touch for a few years. Then, as people do, we drifted apart again. She died of a heart condition in about 1980. There will never be another woman like her—capable, creative, compassionate, and on to me from the get go.

Meanwhile, home had not changed to any great degree…

After I graduated high school, I came back to Virginia and moved back in with Mother and her stuff. She had taken over my sister's old apartment in Falls Church. It was a vast improvement over the dodgy, dirty Arlington model. She still worked nights, mostly, so I saw her briefly in the morning on her way in and my way out to work.

Her first task upon arriving at seven a.m. was to pour a drink, then another, while she pulled together a dinner-like breakfast. Often, her meals involved frying something in oil (tater tots). She maintained a pot of cooking oil on the back of the stove for such meals and would light a fire under the oil soon after arriving home. She would then often go take care of some other task—a shower, a drink, wash dishes, gather and prepare other food, drink, smoke a cig, talk on the phone, drink, read a magazine, and so forth. Sometimes she fell asleep waiting for the oil to heat up.

One afternoon I came home to find six firefighters inside and outside the apartment, going back and forth, discussing what to do, etc. Apparently, Mother had left the oil on, had a few drinks, and went to sleep. Hours later she woke to horrible black smoke filling the house, and a fire raging in her oil pot on the stove. Of course, the natural fire retardants like salt and baking soda were above the stove in a small cabinet, now itself burning and useless. She turned off the gas, but still the fire raged in the pot and still the cabinet doors burned. So she called the local fire station.

The firefighters hit the flames right away with pressurized extinguisher. The cabinets went out, but not the pot. It raged and raged. One of the firefighters, in full protective body and face gear, wearing super thick gloves, finally picked up the pot and carried it outside. He had noticed a break in the sidewalk leading to the apartment. He poured the flaming oil through the crack, into the earth below. The flames shot upward through the hole. That oil resisted repeated use of the fire extinguisher and all attempts to smother it. It raged for another hour before finally cooling enough to put itself out (but not before the firefighters had dumped an impressive amount of sand into the hole for good measure).

Of course, Mother was chagrinned. It was a lucky thing that she did not succumb to smoke inhalation first and burn down the entire building, killing herself and who knows how many others.

About two years later, I moved into that same apartment complex with my soon-to-be husband, Tony, and our adopted dog-child, Schnapps. Ironically, we lived nearly directly across the street from the trailer park my family had moved to when we first came to Virginia. Our neighbors next door included a friend of my brother I had known when I was 10 or 11. He had been a real bully to his own sister, and turned on me one day, trying to strangle me for pestering my brother. I was not happy to see him living upstairs with his wife; however, we both seemed to have grown up, and he seemed to be less of an asshole. Tony and I went fishing with this man and his infantile wife several times. I was never fully comfortable being around him.

Our other neighbors were two young men who smoked a lot of pot, and conspired to organize the May Day Anti-War rallies on the Mall in Washington. Tony and I attended their July 4 anti-war rally with two young cousins. We walked the Mall from end to end enjoying the peace and calm, hippies singing and chanting, gentle protesting. Back up near the History and Technology Museum, we watched while many, maybe one hundred, cops in riot gear and face masks assembled near us, forming a line from Constitution Ave. nearly up to the old castle of the Smithsonian. Within a few minutes a riot was breaking out among the protesters, and cops were lobbing tear gas into the crowd.

Rather than subdue or disperse the protesters, some fell back, but others became enraged with the gas and began to throw rocks and soda bottles at the cops. The cops advanced. The yippies rocked a food truck until it fell over, and threw lit firecrackers at the cops. Down near Constitution Avenue Bob Hope and Dorothy Lamour were practicing their show for the July 4th kickoff to the annual Festival of American Folklife. As tear gas engulfed us, stinging our eyes and burning our armpits, we ran for the car, gasping for air, tearing at our clothes, dabbing our eyes. I could hear Bob and Dorothy singing "I've got you under my skin."

In about 1972, Tony and I decided to start our family, so we rented a large house in Fairfax and Mother took the attic bedroom, which helped us pay rent and her to save a little. Fortunately, Mother kept her "collection" contained within her own room, though the stairs leading up to her room became a kind of crowded filing system of items needing to go up or come down.

I discovered my ability to handle housekeeping on a larger scale, and that picking up after a husband is good training for picking up after children.

I was very pregnant when my brother and three of his friends decided to ride across the country on their bicycles. It took them two months to reach us in Virginia. All four young men "crashed" at our house. On their first night in town, they borrowed my car and drove to D.C. to celebrate (read: get drunk). With at least half a heat on, they came all the way back to our house in the suburbs to drop off one young man, who was too drunk to stand. He was allowed to sleep in my mom's bed upstairs while she was at work.

I woke early in the morning to find feces and vomit all over the main bathroom, plus the stairs and walls going up to my mom's room. He had vomited in her bed as well and since he was not especially adept at wiping his ass while drunk, had left smudges of shit all over the sheets and coverlet, as well.

My brother thought it pretty funny. All four men were laid up that day with severe hangovers. I don't know what that young man thought about when he awoke that morning, but he seemed to have the good sense to be embarrassed.

> **"You have to have some reason to heal."**
>
> —Edgar Cayce

Mother hoarded

In her defense I can state that working nights full time and drinking herself to sleep during the day requires lots of energy. One has no time for mere cleaning and arranging of the home.

Recently, I saw a movie called "Hello, My Name is Doris," about a lonely, grieving older woman who fancies a much younger man. She is also a hoarder. My mother's name is also Doris, and let me tell you: my mother, Doris, makes this Hollywood Doris the Hoarder look like an amateur.

Mother bought a little house in West Virginia, and lived there alone for the last twenty years of her life. If it were possible to pluck the roof off her house and look down into the rooms from above, the piles of the stuff of her life would form a rat's maze: a narrow trail connecting her bathroom to her bed, her bed to the outer room, then to and from the kitchen, to and from the second bedroom and bath, to and from the front and back doors. The walls of her maze built up over time like stalagmites from the steady drip, drop of thoughts and things turned to patterns of thoughts and piles of things, eons of thoughts and rationalizations closing in the spaces as the piles of the stuff grew ever higher and more wall-like.

Stalagmite is a funny word. I looked it up to be sure I was citing the calcium buildup on the *floor* of caves. Shared between *stalagmite* and it's overhead dripping partner, *stalactite*, is the word, *stalag*, which literally means prison. Right. Mother's walls had become her *prison*, her controlled container for capturing all that was not flowing within her and in her life.

After my everything-just-so-sister left home in 1963 I began to see mother's ultra-light housekeeping style, with its occasional insistence upon bleach and scalding water for all the dodgy surfaces—toilets, sinks and some food prep areas—while every other available space became stagnant and burdened with stuff, including the other half of her queen sized bed, piled with "essentials" such as newspapers and magazines, mail, rocks, the likely-reusable someday items, plastic in all it's amazing forms, boxes, bags, clothing parts, empty bottles and cans amid the art projects from old packing materials and egg cartons, film cans filled with wee bits of this and that, her ancient record collection, photos, animal bones and fossils, very old clothes, the clean laundry, various vacuum cleaner parts, dirty dishes and dead potted plants. Mother's hoarding had sprung from certain delusion: control over her environment, meant control of her life.

Looking back, I think she always collected, saved and stored—on every level you can think of. When I was a child she was busy working two jobs, juggling finances (read: kiting checks) and three kids—there was no time to accumulate. When we moved from our Sothern Cal house and began our great road trip, Mother had managed to make lots of our stuff disappear. A few remaining artifacts from her childhood and ours moved East before us. We carried only the necessities that could fit in a 20' X 8' travel trailer.

We lived in that trailer for over a year after we got to Virginia— froze our butts off, too, our first winter. No space to accumulate more than dust and a few treasures purloined from national parks on our six-month cross-country trek.

When we moved into our first apartment in Virginia we had teen-aged Dee, well accustomed to stepping into a motherly role to keep the family moving along, reasonably fed and in only a slight state of disarray. I'm sure we all would have perished from odd fungal infections or rancid food ingestion had Dee not been there, cleaning in self-defense and keeping our larder current.

But Dee escaped early—married "James I" or "Jimmy," at barely 17—and went off to establish her own very clean and orderly home, quickly produce two very clean and orderly children, then just as quickly to move back to California, as neat and clean as you please.

Brent and I were left to hang with Mother. After Dee married, we moved to an even cheaper and more depressing little apartment in a depressed and depressing part of Arlington. There, Mother was free to let life pile up around her. She worked nights now, and Brent and I were largely left to our own devices. No big sister to keep us in line.

We did what we could—doing our own laundry, occasionally breaking down and actually washing dishes, keeping the piles of stuff in our rooms at bay. Brent kept snakes then, too. His room had smelled like a herpetology experiment from an early age. We lived on the second floor and used to tease him about keeping his blinds closed all the time to discourage the prying neighbors in helicopters. For such a lively, bright character as he, his room was mostly dark and airless.

In that old apartment, I shared a room with Mother until I went away to high school in New Jersey. She worked at night, I slept at night; I went to school during the day, she slept during the day. Somehow it worked out. The rare times we were together in that room, I often went to bed much earlier than she. Left to her own devices, night job or no, she would stay up into the wee hours, drinking and playing inside herself. Sometimes she'd cat nap on the couch and not really sleep until mid-afternoon.

Gathering and storing became more serious during this time. Drinking had increased and become a more regular feature of our life together—and smoking, let us not forget the house filled with noxious smoke, the overrun ashtrays, the smoky smell lingering in absolutely everything. As if the apartment had not quite absorbed enough of other people's smoke over the years, Mother felt duty bound to add her share to the walls, rugs, cabinet innards, linens and clothing.

When I came back to Virginia after high school, I moved in again with Mother, who had taken over Dee's old apartment in Falls Church. The 2-bedroom apartment was a vast improvement over the cramped Arlington model. Brent lived in the second bedroom until he was ready to move back to California permanently. I shared a bedroom with Mother again: with her ashtrays mingled with Chanel perfume, her piles of clothes—some laundry, some just left—lining the bedroom walls around the double bed. Plus magazines, mail, crossword puzzles, pens and pencils, shoes and the usual living detritus strewn about making it a bit tricky to get up to pee in the middle of the night.

At first, perhaps, Mother gathered. She became a serious, full time hoarder after moving up to West Virginia as my first husband, Tony, and I moved back to California in 1974.

I heard once that clutter is the way we build monuments to

indecision. Right. What is the clever metaphor one can reach for to understand the steady tidal effect of influx where there is no ebb, no outflow; of filling the perceived void, occupying every available space; of resisting release of what is no longer useful; of becoming so emotionally annealed to one's collections that one must guard against any intrusion, any removal, any offer to help remove, clear, organize or lighten the load. The predictable result of hoarding is that one controls by sheer volume of attachment the quality of life and intimacy with everyone else in the vicinity.

Forgiveness: giving up the hope that the past could be different

Mother was a talker

Lordy, how she could talk, drunk or sober, "til the cows come home and the last dog is dead." A Tower of Babble. She could talk on any subject, often in great detail, anytime, anywhere with anyone, and hold her own. Her stories and monologues were peppered with Southern aphorisms, Biblical sayings and other strange expressions like the two I added to the first sentence of this little rant.

Corralled by Mother, hands and arms waving wildly to illustrate an idea, bystanders were known to back up to avoid being whacked while she talked. If whole-body miming seemed insufficient to underscore her point, Mother simply re-launched her tale to make sure the captive listener got it in full. And, few people could avoid listening, in much the same way one can't *not* look at a train wreck or the replay of JFK being shot in the head.

On good days, sober days, Mother could sometimes sense that the listener had other things to do, other fish to fry, customers waiting, babies crying, bleeding to stanch. She left them laughing and feeling good about themselves. Drunk, no one was safe. She captivated, captured and killed her listening prey with meandering stories, runaway diatribes and droning oratory delivered in slurred and uncertain tones.

My siblings and I could only cringe in horror and embarrassment watching her arm-waving, over-emotional expression, swaying on her feet, as she snared another innocent bystander, their eyes wide, caught like a deer in the headlights of an onslaught of words.

Being so animated and effusive, she was often late to work and other appointments. Leaving the house, leaving other people's houses, getting anywhere on time was damn near impossible. We three monstrous kids often used this side of Mother to avoid going to church. We were going to be late anyway. Inevitably. Sometimes we could forestall the whole business by engaging Mother in stories— what was it that granddad said to you about the chitterlings? Mother would launch into a long recall, eat up lots more time and spare us all the humiliation of church.

Waiting for her to end a conversation was a unique kind of torture. As kids, we begged to go home to our beds, to be released from the agonizing reality of being too young to drive ourselves. We would plead with her and with those she drank with to let us go. But finally going home also meant we had to face her drunken driving to get there.

Talking someone's head off was a way for Mother to connect, to experience a little intimacy. It could also mean she was showing off what she knew of the subject, how she could outsmart the other person, how she never ran out of commentary. You had to be drunk to truly appreciate it.

As she would say, "Don't think it ain't been."

Mother was panicky

"Prone to histrionics." A large part of my childhood I watched help-lessly as my mother "flew off the handle." If she was drunk, her his-trionic displays were apt to be sloppy, degrading, woeful analytical lectures on her sad family and childhood and why she couldn't handle life...or a morose recounting of her life with my mentally ill father. If she was sober, there might be angry outbursts and anxiety attacks.

We kids were embarrassed by her, anxious whenever we were in public together, because she was so anxious in public. She did not know how to end a conversation and would delay others, captivate them. She was always late, anxious about leaving the house and daw-dling until guaranteed to be late, sometimes by more than an hour.

When I was needy, weepy, angry or in any kind of visible distress, my family (led by mom) called me "Sarah Bernhardt." I think Mother had earned the same name in her family. Years later, it's hard to be-lieve that a woman so dismissed in this way by her family, would re-peat such an offence against her own. As a mother, though, I know I have at times let slip the dogs of war against my own children.

We never had a dining room or a dining table in our house. Mother was anxious eating with other people, even her own chil-dren. At restaurants, she would poke and stir at her food, too anxious to simply eat. Her father had been a real tyrant in her youth. After running her down at their dining table, probably drunk and bullying, he would order her to the kitchen to eat with the maids and cooks. She loved to eat in the kitchen. Likely she manipulated in order to be excused to the kitchen. She was never comfortable eating with others.

Being myself in a needy-feeling, anxious state, reminds me of Mother's inability to tolerate, to endure, whatever life circumstance had just unfolded, without anxiety. I learned well not to show my own needs in my relationships, but when pushed, they all come a'tumbling out in very theatrical ways. I also make myself anxious about time, sometimes fritter with time, and get angry at myself for being late or nearly late. I shame myself.

The day I sensed this connection—between my mother's anxiety and histrionics and *my* anxiety—I seemed to calm down inside. I was able to handle many things with ease and focus.

The Walking Man

Mother has a *Walking Man*. I have one, too, in San Francisco, and I suppose they are everywhere if you look for them. The Walking Man appears to be in a trance, or ambling stupor. He is not lost, nor is he out for a stroll, or just down to the store for a pack. He is compulsively walking.

His years of committed drinking swell and flush his face and bloat his reddening hands regardless of his natural skin tone. My Walking Man could be Asian or not, might be thirty to fifty years old: it is difficult to discern his features through the poisoned distortions of his face. I have observed him for about twelve years, his small, quick steps, often talking and gesturing as if signing to underscore a private conversation. He never wanders in areas where other people congest the sidewalks. He is often seen along railway tracks or down avenues welcoming to cars but not to people on foot. I see him several times each month in the outer districts, unvarying in his stride or manner.

If you have ever visited San Francisco, you will never come again without half your winter wardrobe in tow, regardless of what season is playing elsewhere in California. My Walking Man never dresses for wind or fog or rain. Visiting my mother in the eastern panhandle of West Virginia, it never occurred to me that she would have an all-season walker of her own.

"Well, I'll *be*," Mother says, staring up the street.

"What?"

"The Walkin' Man."

I barely have time to recover my senses before she steps out of the car and begins to walk toward him. We have never compared notes on this subject nor discussed this bit of local color. She not only *has* a Walking Man and calls him a "Walking Man," she *knows* him.

"*Now* where's y'mother off to?" Aunt Shep's exasperated voice from the back seat brings me back.

"She's got a Walkin' Man, Shep. There he is."

Shep and I follow Mother's weaving progress from the car, arms waving, calling "Hey, Steve!" Steve, a bloated, red-faced white man, anywhere from thirty-five to fifty years of age, trudges stiffly forward, eyes straight ahead as if seeing nothing. Without contra-lateral arm swing motion, he moves like a robot though somewhat more relaxed. Zombie is more apt.

Mother, determined to wake him, continues to wave her hands and yell. She has to cut right across his path before he stops. In his fixed state, it seems that he does not see, nor want to see her. It takes a few moments for him to pull his attention out of the middle distance and focus on her face, now about six inches from his.

"Haddayadoo, ma'am?" He regards her with dead eyes.

Shep and I gaze in amazement as Mother places a hand on each of Steve's shoulders, gets eyeball to eyeball with him, and tells him he needs help—while she teeters from the wine she consumed this morning so we could leave the house. It was only by Shep's insistence that I was allowed to drive into town.

Shep and I shake our heads—Can you believe it? Mother and the Walking Man sway together on the sidewalk, propped against each other by Mother's outstretched arms, elbows locked to resist his forward tendencies.

Mother admonishes him to get sober, attend AA meetings, and keep his fists out of his wife's face, until somewhere behind his hollow expression, a small recognition dawns and he mutters, "Yes, ma'am, I will."

Finally satisfied or just fatigued, Mother releases her hold and steps to his side. Relieved of the pressure against his shoulders, Steve stumbles forward a few steps then resumes his sleepwalk down the street. Mother regains her balance and strolls back toward the car polishing her knuckles in mock victory. She looks okay for about four steps, until her legs go all woppy-jawed, and one leggy leg crosses too far in front of another and her saunter becomes a dangerous weave. She is forced to make a stride correction or fall down.

Back in the car, Mother treats Shep and me to the confidential story of her Walking Man, his battered spouse and terrified children. She has high hopes for him, though, and believes he will follow her direction toward the nearest AA meeting.

"He just needs to get a few meetings under his belt, he'll be okay," she pronounces.

"Maybe you should take him to a meeting y'self, Doris," Shep offers with a wink to me.

This little vignette typifies my mother's inability to see the absurdity, or possibly arrogance, in being so insistent upon sobriety in another but not for herself. The keys to Steve's life problems could be found by attending AA meetings, but she ignored her own chronic drunkenness.

My mother was one of the kindest people I have ever known, and she abandoned us all for her daily drinking. She could be rational, cautious and caring, and she put us at risk many times because she was drunk. She was a loving person, but not of herself; giving but not *to* herself; seemingly humble, but often proud of her ability to have "handled" people who enabled her addiction and denial. She lied. Her pain, suffering, and life traumas engendered nearly sixty years of self-medication and solace seeking. She conducted a timid relationship with God but nursed a deep craving for grace. As Scott Peck aptly put it, "Alcoholics have a greater thirst for spirit."

She was maddening to live with, yet we loved her. This is the crazy-making, *human* complexity of alcoholism.

Emily had also begun her drinking career by this time. She started early, as I did, though I did not continue drinking. Emily took to alcohol like a fish to water, as is said, to mean she seemed born to drink. When she drank to excess, which was most of the time, all of her pleasant, kind and loving nature seemed to evaporate. She was mean, cold and critical. During one of her rare sober intervals, or a time when she could still conceal her addiction from others, Emily worked for a very posh clothing store in San Francisco. They sent her to Italy, to Milan, to do some schmoozing with designers and buyers. Everywhere she went, every party and fashion show she attended, people offered her wine and other drinks. She protested, she held them off for as long as she could. In those days, Italians knew nothing of "AA" and Em could not convince them that she could *not* drink. Finally, she gave in. In a short time, colleagues who had embraced her were backing away in horror. Emily's Mr. Hyde had shown up and no one was safe. After she returned to the States, her company quietly let her go.

***Mother put herself at risk**, too. After years of being chronically late to work, overselling excuses, missing work from excessive drinking, and so forth, Mother's work supervisor simply did not believe her, or care, that her doctor had taken her off mandatory overtime. So, one night she was forced to work until two in the morning. She promised to "write him up" and complain about the supervisor to the shop steward for ignoring her doctor's orders.*

Dulles Air Mail Facility, at that time, was way out in the middle of Nowhere, Virginia. Mother drove fifty-odd miles or more from her home in West Virginia to go to work every night. On this particular early morning coming home, Mother pulled up to the 7-11 store in Leesburg, Virginia, about 20 miles from the Virginia-West Virginia border, to use the facilities and buy a jug of wine. She talked the attendant's ear off, pausing here and there while some rough looking customers came in for cigarettes and beer. She left the store at about 3:30-ish am to drive the remaining 20 miles or so home.

Two men followed her in a beat up truck. They hailed her with horn and flashing headlights, came alongside in the oncoming lane and shouted and gestured that something was wrong with her rear tire. She pulled over and got out. The man in the passenger seat of the truck got out and forced her at gunpoint back into her car. She was to follow the truck, ask no questions and not look at him.

Too late. Mother had already gotten a good look. Being an artist, she had registered in less than 5 seconds everything about his face that would later convict him.

They drove to a church a few miles up the road. There were no lights in the parking area in front of the old church, no lights anywhere. Mother was instructed to take off her clothes and lie in the grass. She pleaded her case as a mother and grandmother, was thrown to the ground by the man who had forced her to drive to this place, and was threatened again that she would die. She remembered lying in the cool grass looking up at the stars. She worried for us kids and the grandkids knowing their mother and grandmother had died like this, but also thought if the stars were the last she would ever see of this life, it would be okay.

The second man could not be seen in the extreme darkness. He rifled her purse and the car for valuables, and oddly, dropped her keys on the floor of the car, driver's side.

The men took turns raping and sodomizing her. Or attempting to. The older man simply could not perform and blamed her. Mother's bowels let loose from shock and fear; the younger man seemed to enjoy slopping around in her warm excrement. Finally, they left her. She lay still in the grass for a while looking at the stars. Still here. She was sixty-three.

She got up first to hands and knees and slowly felt around for her clothes. A shirt. Nothing else. She felt for the car and crawled into the driver's seat. She had begun to shake and it took several minutes to get into her shirt. Looking for other clothing and shoes in the dim dome light of the car, she found the keys!

Severely shaking now, she somehow managed to drive back into Leesburg, right up to the door of the sheriff's office. She was not sure she could walk, and had no clothes below the shirt so she laid on the horn until some officers came out to help her. Mother was given a blanket but nothing else—no water either because she would have to go to the hospital and be probed for evidence, her body now a crime scene.

The officers were kind and understanding but they had to get information before she could go to the hospital. Mother was in shock, having difficulty describing her assailants, so she grabbed an envelope off the deputy's desk, was handed a pencil, and quickly sketched a likeness of the first man. The officers passed the sketch around the room. They all knew him immediately: Jonny Mack Orr.

Two hours later, at dawn, after every orifice had been swabbed and samples taken, a woman arrived with a new bathrobe and slippers, a little ditty bag with soap, shampoo, powder, toothbrush and toothpaste, and a comforting smile. Irene had come within thirty minutes of being notified by the Sheriff's office. Irene was the Victim-Witness Program Coordinator for Loudon County. She and Mother would become friends for life.

After being allowed to bathe and brush her teeth, with Irene close at hand if needed, the Sheriff himself came to ask a few more questions. They had arrested Jonny Mack Orr, and his younger cousin, but they needed to know anything she could tell them about the second man. They were sure the cousin was the second man; he had been in trouble with Orr before. They could have proved it if DNA tests had been widely available and accepted. Unfortunately, Mother could not identify him because she did not see him, nor did he speak during her ordeal.

Before the trial, Mother created a better, more detailed drawing of Jonny Mack Orr. She told the Judge that she wasn't completely sure of the expression she had drawn. "I am accustomed to drawing children and nice people," she explained. Orr was quickly convicted of kidnapping, rape, sodomy and robbery, and a few other felonies, and sentenced to 70 years. The Sheriff told my brother that he would personally make sure the convicts at Lorton Men's Reformatory would know that Mr. Orr was a grandmother-rapist.

As soon as she was able, Mother joined the Victim-Witness Program with Irene as her guide. She worked as an artist for other victims of violent crimes. And she came to the aid of other battered and raped women with a bathrobe, slippers and toiletries, and the kind of compassion and acceptance only a woman can bring to another woman in such a situation.

Mother retired early, attended intensive therapy and joined victim groups, but she was wrecked in a way she would never fully recover from. Her drinking increased and was not confined to particular times or places or volumes.

The Sheriff and his officers held her in high esteem, especially because of her work with Irene and her willingness to be with victims through court appearances and the worst of it. But they also knew she was an alcoholic and that she often drove intoxicated through their jurisdiction on her way home.

About a year after her case completed and her assailant jailed, Mother bragged to me about how nice the Sheriff's deputy had been to escort her to the state line. She had been drinking in Arlington at my aunt's house and was getting really tired on the long ride home. They pulled her over after midnight, for weaving, made sure she was awake, then escorted her to the West Virginia line, about 20 miles away. She still had another 5 miles of winding country roads up to her house, and would have to get there by the grace of God.

Next day, I called the Sheriff and read him the riot act. If he or his deputies ever caught her driving drunk through Loudon County again they should treat her like any other DUI citizen: arrest her and let her sleep it off in jail—or else I would personally hold him responsible. I hated to be so rude knowing the younger Sheriff was about my age and was really supportive of anything my mother wanted from his office. But she could have killed herself or someone else by driving drunk or falling asleep at the wheel.

The Sheriff called my mother that same day and told her that her daughter had just dressed him down and if she was going to drink and drive in his county, he was now under orders to take her in, no more coddling. Mother was furious with me, and embarrassed, because she could no longer hide out in denial and she knew it.

Through the Victim-Witness program Mother directed wife-batterers, DUIs and many potentially dangerous drunks into AA meetings. By the time she attended *her* first AA meeting, she walked into a room full of people who already knew her and were ready to welcome her to sobriety. She had six sober years under her belt before she died.

Mother died in 1991. Her memorial took place in a tiny rural church just off Route 9 on the road up to her old home. It took me two solid weeks to clean out the house, bag up mountains of garbage and haul off items to donate. The Doris Booth Memorial Yard Sale, same day as her memorial, included some items that had been in her yard for those two weeks with a sign begging anyone to carry away whatever could be hauled. We filled much of the front yard of the church with tables of all kinds of stuff—household stuff, kitchen stuff, war memorial stuff, antiques and junk. We gave away her old 78rpm record player and a big stack of 78s. My antiques-dealer aunt sifted through the old stuff that my brother, sister and I did not know what to do with. My cousin took the war memorabilia. I gave away the antique furniture to one of her best friends and shipped great boxes of stuff to California for re-distribution to my brother and sister and our kids.

Inside the church I set up a memorial table, with Mother's ashes in a box behind a poster collaged with photos of her from different ages, and with various friends and family. At nine a.m., friends filed in to pay respects. People my mother's older sister would not have sought company with, folks who seemed to her like low country trash, spoke eloquently about Mother—how she had encouraged them to get to their first AA meeting, how they recognized her as a "lady" with class and poise, a kind-hearted friend and confidant, a caring person, on and on. My aunt was duly impressed. After a brief meditation we chatted with snacks and told a few tales.

An hour later we officially opened the yard sale and throughout that day moved about a half ton of her stuff on to other people's houses and lives. At the end, when none of us could stand any longer, I packed up the car, stuffing every available space, and drove off to Charles Town, where the big Goodwill dumpster awaited the final donation.

My mother was quite a character: well known to many for her southern gentility, her enthusiastic talkativeness, her generosity and courage, and occasionally, wisdom. She had been a volunteer with the Loudon County, Virginia Victim/Witness program for four years before she found the courage to stop her own drinking. By then, through her work with the county, she had influenced a dozen or more alcoholic men and women, including her "Walking Man" (pg. 78), to sober up. By the time she attended *her* first AA meeting, she walked into a room full of friends.

All there is, is this instant and God has posed one question that we all must answer: Do you want to be one with all eternity? And our lives are about moving from "no thank you" to yes. Our entire life construct is about "no thank you" and we don't wake up until we say yes.

—Author unknown

CHAPTER 2: Denial: A River in Egypt or Don't Even kNow I Am Lying

Denial is the cornerstone that anchors the state of mind of an alcoholic, enabling them to rationalize the need (the addiction) to drink. Alcoholics lie to themselves, and anyone else who will buy into their twisted logic, about their drinking amounts and frequencies, their own capacity for rational thought, and when drunk, how much control they have over speech, movement, driving and many other aspects of life. There's a mountain of stuff they do not attend to because drinking has become more important: health and wellness, family unity and needs, spousal needs, marital vows, common sense and safety, work, deadlines, promises, goals and responsibilities. Denial and lying are but two channels alcohol uses to talk through the addict. If an alcoholic can claim he or she has not ever missed a day of work due to drinking, it becomes the primary proof of their ability to control the use of their substance, regardless of the effects elsewhere in their life and relationships.

I can stop anytime I want.

I can have a beer once in a while…

I go to work every day.

I live in a nice home, I have a job…

I don't drink in the morning.

Alcohol keeps me from being depressed.

I wouldn't have any fun without a drink.

I need it to calm down.

It settles my stomach.

Billy joe used all of the above lines, or "rational lies," to deny his problem with alcohol for a good long time.

Billy Joe and I were friends for nearly forty years. He was a sober alcoholic for at least fifteen years before we met. He and his brother, Haywood, grew up in Texas. When he was nearly six and his brother four, BJ's mother dropped them off as she often did, at their grandmother's house. The kids went to the front window, just like many times before, and watched and waved as their mother drove off. She never returned for them.

Billy Joe said his mom "just had to go out and be-bop and boogie," his way of saying she liked to party, drink all night with men and have fun. Two little kids interfered with her preferred lifestyle. They were raised by their grandmother, whom they called "Momma."

Momma was churchgoing, stern and loving. She was clear about expectations for their school performance, homework and chores. BJ and Haywood got music lessons. BJ went to music school. Haywood went off to college a year after Billy Joe joined the Navy as a musician in the Navy Band.

In the Navy, Billy Joe learned to drink. He took to it naturally, and too well. Whenever he and his buddies were let out of their controlled environment, they went straight to the bars to drink. This pattern had them staggering back to base nearly every weekend. One morning, BJ woke in a wet stench. Half his pillow and face, and his boots next to the bed—all drenched in vomit. With extra horror he realized that it was not his own, but had been delivered during the night by the man in the bunk above. BJ decided from then on to grab a top bunk.

He would have been a career Navy man, but the Vietnam War threatened to put him on a ship and send him to the combat zone. He retired so he could drink without interruption for several more years. Visiting Momma was not easy during those years because he did not want to go without a drink for more than a day. She did not approve, and had locked him out of the house a few times.

BJ fell in and out of relationships. Moved from time to time, changed jobs often, and did not seem to be able to find work as a studio musician, which had been his dream. Alcohol had become central to his life and his dream just got further away. As they say in the music business, he lost his chops.

Around the time he realized he could no longer cut it as a studio musician, he remembers meeting a rather pathetic old man with nothing but hospital issue gown on his back, who told him that he had left the hospital because he needed a drink. "Needed a drink more than he needed food, medicine or housing," he told me. Not long after that he remembers going out with some drinking buddies and being drunk most of the night. Next morning he couldn't find his car to get to work. The light was beginning to seep in.

He decided to go to an AA meeting with a sober friend. After the meeting, BJ was thirsty. "Let's get a beer," he suggested. The look on his friend's face said it all. "You mean, I can't have a *beer* once in a while? I can have a beer once in a while…are you kidding? Naw, come on…" Billy Joe thought there was a real difference between drinking beer and drinking the hard stuff. He "fell off the wagon" a few more times after that, but only for a weekend or a few days. He finally admitted he was powerless over alcohol, went into more conscious recovery and never drank again.

From my diary, about 1995:

She's gone again. Just like that. Her hold on sobriety is so thin and fleeting. She has disappeared into her addiction again, lying her way in and around her family and her "sobriety house," lying her way into deeper embrace with her substance of choice.

My sister, says "It's like she has the whole family's genetic load for addiction." She seems to carry it for the family. We seem to all have the marks of generations of addicts before us—an imprimatur of trauma and dysfunction, and the genetic predisposition toward gross unconsciousness. Some families pass on the cancers, heart diseases, gout or obesity. We have the alcohol disease. Our family also carries and passes on various other forms of addiction: righteous indignation, self-doubt, superiority, resentment, being right and first, denial in all its tones and temperaments.

Emily, one of the brightest, sweetest, coolest, most capable and with the curse of huge potential, is the one most afflicted in the category of alcohol. So poisoned, that like Nathaniel Hawthorne's "Rappaccini's Daughter," she can't live long without it. Years and years of recovery homes and sobriety programs, and yet she is ever lured back into drinking. She is not a nice, friendly drunk like my mother. Her Mr. Hyde is surly and coarse.

Does she in some way carry the lion's share of the family drinking gene? Is she the end of this terrible lineage factor, or just a helpless and unlucky harbor for deep family brokenness?

Lena (Emily's daughter) called me today to tell me the news. Her mother disappeared again, lied about why the recovery center kicked her out, and about her status with the rehab staff. Lena is eight. She needed to talk to family. Something in her urges her to talk about it and my sister (her grandmother) does not stand in the way. Lena holds both confusion and compassion for her mother, and with perhaps only a fraction of insight about her mother's effect on her own sense of self. At least, I tell my sister, she is learning that she can call someone, she can reach out when she needs to, perhaps a credit to her grandmother's good sense to have her in therapy, to encourage her to talk about her life. A hard lesson for Lena is that she cannot trust either parent at their word. They are both, I hope not hopelessly, addicted not only to substances, but also to the drama and mental/emotional games and power plays that go with the disease of denial.

I continue to pray. I don't know if it helps, and I can't know if it doesn't help, so I will continue to pray. I'm feeling a bit guilty today because I don't remember to pray every damn day, nor have I written as often as I have thought to write to Emily to tell her to stay and pray with me. Damn procrastination and busyness. I want to do those things, like write letters, and I just don't get to it as often as I think I should. I believe each of us can make a difference, an impact, and so I feel guilty because I might have said or done something that would have encouraged her to stay and pray and work her program. The portion of the alcohol disease visited upon the sober codependent family like me, is the nagging sense that "if only..." and that we all must be diligent in our effort to pray, to serve, to communicate, or all may be lost in an instant.

As with my elders, if those I love die before I have done all I can do to let them know how much I love them and care about them, then I am left with a horrible regret. Regrets kill self-trust. With only a few elders left standing, I do not care to make any more regrets, they pile up too quickly as it is.

In her late 60's, Lena's grandmother, my sister, became an alcoholic like her daughter and our mother. She, too, is mean and critical of others, imperious, and after ten years of steady drinking, impervious.

Alcoholism is a family disease. My brother and I seemed to have escaped the addiction, but no one escapes the traumas, confusion, grief and loneliness of the disease, the humor and horror of alcoholism.

Ben, the gun, the cat and Emil

"Emil" is my choice of pseudonym, borrowed from the humorous horror stories told by Justin Wilson, outlandishly funny Cajun storyteller, detailing his drunken adventures with his friend Emil; say "ay-MEEL" like you mean it, southern style.

A friend of my sober roommate tells this one: Ben and his buddy, Emil are putting back a case of beer one day at Ben's house. They wash down the beer with some Irish whiskey, and smoke a few joints, too, just to keep it lively. While they party, Ben's daughter's cat begins to yowl. The cat's yowling starts to interfere with a good day's drunk.

The more the men drink, the louder and more obnoxious the cat seems to be. They start weaving a story to account for the cat's crying, her distress becoming a real drag on their fun. The more they drink, the more sinister their cat story becomes. They decide that the cat is ill and is dying, these yowls must be its last attempt to get help for a condition surely to be lethal, though not quickly enough for their liking.

They drink some more and consider their predicament. The cat is likely too far gone to benefit from an expensive trip to the animal hospital. No, the only sensible thing to do is to put the cat out of its misery.

Ben gets his .357 Magnum and loads up. Emil grabs the cat and they go out to the backyard to dispatch the deathly ill cat to her maker. Emil holds the cat, while Ben takes aim. Both men are swaying wildly, barely able to stand, let alone be still. The gun lazily tracks the gyrating motion of the cat Emil is trying his best to hold at arms-length in front of his own swaying body. The cat, having had enough of this nonsense, writhes and scratches, trying to bite Emil until he can stand it no longer and drops her just as Ben fires the Magnum. It is by pure luck that Emil survives with a bullet in his thigh. The cat is clean away.

Ben realized later that most of the time Emil had held the cat directly in front of his own body, and had he been able to aim properly, the bullet would have sailed through the cat and killed Emil right there in the backyard. This little adventure not only sobered him up in the moment, but encouraged Ben to get to an AA meeting forthwith.

What the heart loves is the cure.

—African prover

One of the principal drunken writings about the phenomenon of writers and drinking was created by Charles Jackson, the alcoholic who in 1944 wrote the novel, The Lost Weekend, also made into a hugely popular movie by Billy Wilder, starring Ray Milland as the drunken writer."

From Drinking in America: Our Secret History, by Susan Cheever

The Lost Weekend

When I lived in San Francisco, there was a bar near the beach on Taraval Street named "The Lost Weekend." The stucco exterior sported a 1950's appendage that stuck out from the building, a long triangular thing with three "holes" or perhaps bubbles in it. Maybe the building used to be a laundromat. Maybe it was born a bar.

I scoffed at this place for many years: how could someone name a bar after a depressing movie about alcoholism? The very idea was appalling to me. One evening on my way to the beach with a friend, I challenged her to go with me into this bar, into this hard liquor-serving place with the bad name, to see just what kind of place it really was, who drank there and how cruddy it could be. We entered with trepidation but ready to judge what we saw and heard.

To our surprise, the denizens of the Lost Weekend bar were friendly, local souls who came for a cocktail or a beer and to listen to music. It was a small place, dimly lit in the interior, most light coming from behind the bar, the barman's workspace and the recess above it. We took a table in a dark corner and watched. We ordered black-and-tans. Some folks seated at the bar turned and greeted us. No one looked drunk and disorderly: quite the contrary.

After a few minutes, a very large man squeezed himself into the seat of a Hammond organ perched on a platform above and behind the bar, in a small neon violet-lit alcove. He played very well—all music from the 1940's and 50's. An older couple got up to dance, a few people sang the lyrics, laughter and smiles and conversation all around without being too loud. No slurred, slushy behavior, no drunken routs, nothing to judge or to put down. My friend and I were impressed to say the least. Maybe there really *is* such a thing as "social drinking."

Perhaps sad to say, The Lost Weekend bar faded and closed some years later. But while it livened up the quiet end of Taraval Street, I smiled whenever I passed by.

"It has been said that alcohol is a good servant and a bad master", wrote Christopher Hitchens in an essay— "The Muse of Booze"— on the famous drinking writer Kingsley Amos.

PART II:

Finding Courage and Compassion

CHAPTER 3: Awakening to my self

I am not an alcoholic. I can't hold enough to qualify, and what I do drink goes to my head way too fast. I used to call myself a "cheap date."

I am addicted to the alcoholic, which is to say I am deeply imprinted with the notion that I am somehow responsible for my mother's drinking and somehow hold the key to her sobriety—if only I can say the right things, believe strongly enough, do enough for her, show her the way— she will be able to quit drinking and go back to being my mother again.

Needless to say, I have allowed her addiction to become central in my life, have twisted my self-concept around to help her heal her own. So, in Recovery, there is much to acknowledge, a big mess to unravel in order to find myself again, to redirect my energy into my own life and endeavors, and to learn healthy ways of relating and loving. Here is a little of what I have learned about myself while traveling the road of recovery.

Common characteristics of children of alcoholics:

- **low self-esteem (often to do with abandonment)**

- **sense of emptiness (the giving up hope aspect of aban-donment)**

- **eating disorders (anxiety and feeling endangered from abandonment)**

Life in the Forest of Self Recognition

Coming out of the woods, I see I never left home, never felt like a grown up with *boundaries*, whatever that means. The only boundaries I know are at the feet of trees marking a territory, protecting an underground communication system linking all growing things to each other and to the community of the forest.

I am a 12-year old when it comes to relationships. My immature expectations blind me to how people display their natures over and over again, while I'm searching their faces for recognition and caring. Too long I stay with the old, the safe, the known path, walking that path into a deeper rut, regardless of its inevitable turnings and twistings in the wood, and without remembering that my path leads inevitably to the same invisible cliff, overhanging the same inevitable chasm. I forget to notice whether the person I am seeking love from is capable of giving love or worthy of receiving from me.

I have weak self-care muscles, I put the other first in my life, wrap my searching vines around the other's pain, his passion and preferences. I fear the new and different, and so will try to detain or arrest the changing seasons, the falling leaf that signals the shift in light, in nutrient, in moisture, within the closed system I am growing with the other.

I keep myself to myself, protected and out of the air and sun. I am blind to those who would manipulate my tender feeling fronds, bend them toward their own needs and desires, train them to cling to a nature unlike my own.

I have to remember that my recovery matters. It needs to matter to me, to ride alongside any life decision, venture or trajectory. It does not need to be central, rather it needs to inhabit the quiet undergrowth in my life, informing and inspiring me to go deeper into every situation or behavior, to pay attention around the edges of my life.

In the inner sanctums of an unhealthy forest, guilty loyalty to the poisoned garden that addicted us becomes the norm, the canopy reducing all available light, holding the air in stifling closeness. Creatures abound. Meat eaters, scavengers, vultures, and various lichens glean by osmosis all available untainted sustaining fluids to maintain their hold on life.

As a co-dependent I have become a wary creature: I walk the darkening glades on tiptoe so as not to waken the hidden, baiting beasts; wait for the right time, the rotting of the 'hide' I myself have built. I watch for the signs of both danger and safety; rehearse my escape and gather resources until I feel the least little strength to finally run from home, leave the abusive partner, say no or say yes, finally, to what is right for me and promises to move me forward.

Self-advocacy does not come easily. "Practice makes progress" I hear in Al-Anon meetings. I salve my terror of needing anything from anyone with phrases designed to support my newly budding self-awareness: Easy Does It, Give it Up, Pray for the SOB. If I am serious in recovery, I do not trust my own longing for love—giving or receiving. I must wait in sheltered coves of new, uncertain ways of being, until I understand what it means to *let the right one in*: the beneficence of a caring Universe offering support and provision to anything I genuinely desire.

So much love left on the table; so much kindness ignored or unseen, unfelt, disbelieved...saying Thank You and meaning it; or hearing Thank You and taking it in.

Progress vs Perfection

When I was eleven I did not know how to speak to my mother about her drinking without being angry, moody or critical. The backlog of personal complaints, unfulfilled needs and confused messages was just too heavy. I got sucked into circular arguments that started with her attempt to get to the bottom of my truancy and run-away tendencies but always came unerringly back around to *her* problems, her unfulfilled life, her sorrows. During one particular argument that was clearly heading down the same rat hole, I slammed the iron down onto the shirt I was punishing and declared her a "fucking alcoholic" at the top of my lungs. She slapped my face.

Many years later, following confinement in a high school for "wayward" girls, a "date-rape" pregnancy, therapy, early marriage, divorce, second marriage, second divorce, therapy, more children, therapy, Al-Anon, meditation, distance, and time, lots of time…something had shifted in me. At thirty-six I sat at her table listening to the old story of how she had no money, why she could not be helped and how desperate she was for help, and I just did not feel like spending my precious life force energy arguing. I turned to her and said in a clear voice, in my best matter-of-fact manner, "You have a drinking problem. Until your drinking problem is handled, until you are living sober, we can't even begin to solve these other problems. No use talking about them." And turned back around to my sandwich.

I could see her out of the corner of my eye, winding up her arms, getting ready to spew in histrionic anger, go dramatic or ballistic or fly off in some other direction. Then, just as quickly as the storm had risen, she let out a long sigh and her balloon of denial deflated. From then on, I imperfectly set boundaries in the same matter-of-fact, direct way.

No, I'll drive. You have been drinking. I will drive or I will not go.

Do not call me if you have been drinking. Period.

I'm leaving in 10 minutes with or without you.

I've already heard that (excuse, story, reasoning, assumption…).

You know the solution for that.

Hmmm. What are you going to do about that?

No thanks.

No, I do not wish to drink with you.

I am finished listening now.

You drunk is not interesting or fun for me. I'm going to…

I am not going to let you be in charge of that.

No, that's me taking care of myself, me being responsible for my life.

No, that's *not* about you; it's about me.

No, that's about *you*; that's not about me.

It took years, and much work on myself, to say these kinds of things without malice, without anger or any room left for misinterpretation. Subtlety has no impact with alcoholics, and can be taken as being on their "side." I learned to accept being an adult but not my mothers' parent, and to know I would never be a child again, she would never be able to take care of me. Now to preserve my own life and sanity, I also had to learn to be direct, authentic and clear. And to be willing to let go. I continue to learn and work on it today.

Sometimes you have to soak the beans all night.

Dry Drunks

Dry drunk behavior can run the gamut from lethal to trusting and caring. I briefly dated a man in recovery who was polite and funny, seeming thoughtful and kind. During the time I knew him, I went through a period of injury/illness that produced bouts of terrible fatigue and affected my ability to think clearly. I explained this situation to him early on, and often had to decline invitations to go out if I felt one of these episodes coming on. He seemed willing to be accommodating, seemed to want to help, be useful, to bring food or entertainment to me.

I began to notice in my weakest moments he slipped in some criticism or challenge that I could only weakly defend. In my clear, strong moments he dodged my questions and avoided talking about the "little bombs" he had dropped while I was down. He consistently ignored his responsibility in the dis-connected moments, preferring self-effacing remarks and false humility.

In dry drunk behavior there is always denial, avoidance and dishonesty or, at least, a lack of transparency. Active alcoholics and dry drunks may turn their denial toward their partner, manipulating or "Gaslighting"* so the unwary co-dependent feels responsible for the behavior the alcoholic refuses to acknowledge.

But it takes two to tango, as the saying goes. I do not create these situations alone; no one person is responsible for the nest of entanglement that is co-dependency. I wish and hope for us all and each to be reasonably self-aware and self-assessing, open our eyes to our co-created relationships.

Equally necessary, though difficult, is the idea of calling them out in their behaviors without taking it personally, without trying to fix or overly educate or shame the dry drunk. I must remember that I have moments or periods of unconsciousness, too, in relationship. Misfires are never all and only about the *other*. And, Co-dependents can also exhibit or act out dry drunk behavior, too.

*In the 1944 film "Gaslight" Charles Boyer plays the master manipulator of his young wife, played by Ingrid Bergman. Set at the turn of the twentieth century, when gas was the mode of lighting, the murderer-husband sows seeds of insanity in his wife's mind, to distract her from noticing his nightly rummaging for her aunt's jewels in the attic. The gaslight in her parlor dips down after he leaves the house and returns to normal intensity just before he comes back from his nightly search. She begins to doubt herself, and because he has slyly confined her to the house, and played her by hiding things and lying, she begins to lose her mind. Hence, the phrase, *gaslighting*.

"A person looking for a healthy relationship concentrates on cultivating within himself or herself the qualities that another high-quality person would find lovable."

Terry Gorski, founder of *Cenaps* and an internationally recognized expert on substance abuse and recovery.

Relationship (aka: wow, have I got a lot to learn...)

I was desperate to make friends. I was desperate to make a good impression, to force popularity by trotting out a mask self, a persona that could "bond" quickly before anyone found out I lacked anything, or that I came from a shamefully embarrassing family, or saw I was damaged and flawed. I was so hungry to make friends I hardly noticed if the people I pushed myself on were worthy themselves.

My pattern of over-selling myself, attaching, and then realizing what I had attached to, propelled me into quick commitments and even marriages. I seemed to leap from being acquaintances to a commitment without noticing the steps between that could help me learn about the other person and consider my own safety and security.

I began to notice that "my mask self" had simply found another mask self to play with. It wasn't long before I was looking for an exit strategy. Some of those relationships required years of stress, doubt, abuse, neglect and confusion before I found the door. Attending Al-anon, working on the inside, allowed me to see my patterns more clearly.

Terry Gorski, lecturer and trainer in the world of alcoholic recovery, identifies important formative *stages* in relationships: casual relating, companionship, friendship, and functional associations (people making a conscious decision to handle some aspect of life in a committed way, whether with romance or in a purely business capacity).

Terry Gorski, excerpted from an Article: "What Is A Healthy Relationship?" by Linda Atkins (sorry, I do not know where this was originally published).

> *"Don't think that casual and superficial relationships have anything to do with love or commitment. Take your time, let it grow. Get to know the other person, to see if you are dealing with a safe, sane one. Who are you with this person: open, curious, relaxed, anxious, withholding, too scared, equal?"*

Honesty and Awakening

I met George in San Francisco at the Salvation Army store where he worked. He was handsome, charming, smart and strong. I was immediately attracted to him and would have invited him home that day, but decided to play coy. I continued visiting the store to look for furniture and other items, while privately hoping to "run into" him.

At first, I did not realize he worked there not only as a job, but because he was in alcoholic recovery, living at the Salvation Army men's center across the street. Even knowing that, it did not sink in and I did not have enough education in recovery to know the implications and possibilities of involvement with a newly recovering alcoholic.

The fast story of our lives: We dated a few times, and then he came home to my bed. We had a child together, moved in together and tried to make a life together. Toward the end of our relationship, about seven years in, my mother died.

I had been with her for about two weeks before her death and six months later went back to clear out her house for quick sale. Around the one-year anniversary of her death, the loss of her came back to me with a compounded force. Though I felt fairly clear with Mother toward the end of her life, and had let her go without reluctance, I had not completed my grieving.

At that time I felt isolated from George, unable to sense any affection or honesty between us. I did not like the person I had become—anxious, suspicious, angry and vigilant. I did not like the person he seemed to become—distant, withdrawn, involved elsewhere and disinterested in home life and our son. My grieving further isolated me from him.

I tried to talk with him about it, but he was not available. In one of my deepest, despairing moments, I slipped down to my home office where I could cry in private, and not wake our son. George knocked on the door and when I opened it, proceeded to express his anger at me, for my odd behavior toward him. "I'm grieving for my mother. This is not about you," I yelled at him.

It was an awkward first step out of my insane thinking it was normal for me to give all my energy, life and focus to the other person, that I should come last on my list. It was the first time I simply told the truth without varnishing, avoiding, or withholding vital information about *me*.

The alcoholic thinks it's all about him; the co-dependent acts as if he's right, it *is* all about him. Whenever Mother and I tried to get at the truth, no matter what predicament I was suffering through, the subject would always come back around to *her* failure and confusion, her losses, her pain and grief. At that time I simply was not equipped, in spite of all my marvelous training and years of therapy, to know in the moment what I was sensing and feeling inside me.

We paid a high price to
Cleve to our broken mothers and fathers
They who went away inside
When abandonment ended their childhoods too soon.
We mourn their lost minds and broken hearts,
Yet we have stayed too long, as well
Accommodated.
Deep pockets formed for carrying losses
We deferred self-knowing
Abandoned joy and needs,
And tried to flower elsewhere.

**Humility is learning what I
already know the hard way.**

—Me

Children of alcoholics often feel crippled by co-dependence, though in the natural world, co-dependence or interdependence is the only way to live, and how nature, and perhaps humanity, continues to thrive. Co-dependence has become the byword indicating the depth of our loss of self to the other, to the system we were born into, and the "unit of horror" we are trying to grow out of to reach this healthier vista of *inter*dependence.

Chapter 4: Rippin' n Runnin'

A brief history of drugs…

**"The best thing about being older is that I did all
my stupid shit before the internet." —Anon**

ONE NIGHT I RODE IN A CAR with my friend, her brother and
his two pals. They gave us beer. I was twelve. We drove around some
areas of Arlington, Virginia completely unknown to me. We listened
to the radio, sang songs, laughed, and drank. The boys mostly talked to the boys and Annie and I talked with each other. As I drank I
became sleepy, my speech sloppy; my face had an odd numb feeling
and my hands and feet were swollen. Soon I would really need to pee.

We couldn't find a place with a bathroom and were miles from
anyone's house—none of us wanted to go near our own house anyway, our parents would know we were all drunk.

Someone decided that I could step outside the car and pee. Boys
do it all the time. Problem was, I could not stand up. Once my feet
were on the ground, I could not control the swaying and weakness in
my legs. I ended up peeing while sitting on the curb. Laughing and
dismayed by my own lack of control, I did manage to not drench myself, but was embarrassed by not being able to stand or walk.

I drank one beer within an hour or so and was so drunk I could not stand or walk, could not express myself, could not feel my body and had no idea where I was or if I would ever get home. No control over my body meant I would not be able to control what happened to me. My fun night with beer became a nightmare I could not wake from. Though nothing evil or violent happened to me that time, I have little memory of the experience, except of the swift change in my sense of self upon realizing how helpless I had become.

In my senior year, my brother wrote to tell me that my first boyfriend died. Lindsey and I were sweet on each other in seventh grade! My brother knew his sister. Definitely the first and probably the last innocent love of my life.

Apparently, Lindsey's parents gifted him with a new sports car for graduating early from high school and being accepted at Georgetown U. He and a friend went out one-night drinking and driving. They flew down the Whitehurst Freeway coming into Georgetown, top down, having a time. They took the off-ramp that spirals up to the Key Bridge where Lindsey lost control of the car and it climbed over the three-foot concrete retaining wall and dropped the car and the two boys into the Potomac River.

Every year I adorn my Christmas tree with a small stuffed bunny Lindsey gave me at Easter over fifty years ago.

And, Jack, an all-star football player, handsome, kind and friendly, smart, a great life ahead of him. We all loved him, and even younger girls like me would blush in his presence.

Coming back from a football game with too many kids piled into a VW beetle, the driver lost control and flipped the car. Jack was thrown out of the roof hatch and the car came down on him. He likely died when he hit the pavement. As they say in the papers, alcohol was involved.

I tried marijuana a few times in my late teens while still in Virginia. But it wasn't until my late twenties that I tried anything else from the ever-expanding drug menu of the late 70's and early 80's. After a year of working in downtown San Francisco, I decided to try to find a job nearer home. A new café opened in my neighborhood and I did everything in my power to impress the new owner and force him to say yes and try me out. I pulled espresso in that café for over two years, meeting the local hipsters, hippies, poets and musicians. They all "did" some kind of drugs.

Back in '68, when I came back home to Virginia from high school, I ran into an old middle school pal. He asked me what did I *do* and I had no idea what he was talking about. In fact, I was shocked to find out that he smoked pot, dropped acid and took pills and god-knows-what all the time. He thought I was a prude and totally out of it; I thought he was an idiot to take such risks with his mental health.

But in my late twenties, having missed much of the hippie era I grew up in, I felt ready to find out what it was all about. My husband and I had split up, I had my own apartment and our daughter stayed with her dad's family half the time. Much of my social life revolved around the café and its varied and interesting customers. I smoked pot and listened to music. I met some local musicians (who went on to be quite famous) and we smoked and listened to jazz-fusion and experimental electronic music.

A year or so into this new life, I decided to share a house with a girlfriend and her kids. She was no stranger to drugs. In that house, I tried cocaine and LSD for the first time. There were other drug opportunities, of course—black beauties, valium, psilocybin mushrooms, speed, dexies and even heroin—but I wasn't able to handle much in the way of alcohol or drugs, my body simply could not process very fast and I got drunk or high very quickly. I used to laugh about it and call myself a "cheap date."

Funny thing about drugs: when you are into the scene, drugs are everywhere! Everyone has something to share or to sell. While living in Glen Park, I met most of the major drug users and dealers in that small neighborhood. At every dinner party somebody was drawing out lines of coke on a mirror, or on the porcelain top of a toilet tank; or pulling out a pipe or some joints. After the café closed for the night, weed and wine were readily available to help with the clean-up. The café owner and his wife invited me to my very first Passover Seder. Hard to believe now, but we got stoned *before* the rituals and meal. I have almost no memory of the Seder.

My café job alone could not adequately support me. I asked a couple of guys who played chess in the café about painting houses with them during the day to make more money. Thus began a part-time and later full-time career in the trades. If I thought my little neighborhood was up to its armpits in drugs, everyone I met through house painting and the trades seemed to be on something or dealing something.

While working as a painter, I was routinely offered weed, beer, sometimes coke, and use of the hot tub. It usually meant the owner wanted to have sex with me. Trust me when I tell you, turning down drugs is easier than having to back pedal and get out of there when you're already high.

One day I came home early from a day of painting with just enough time to shower and change my clothes before I picked up my daughter from school. The door was dead-bolted—locked out! I knocked, but my roommate, Jude, would not come to the door. She may have thought I would go away, but I knew alternate routes into the house. I stepped over our porch rail onto the down-street side neighbor's roof, and tiptoed back to our downstairs bathroom window. Once in, I casually walked upstairs to my room and shower. I heard Jude in the parlor talking with some men. Smoke filled the lower hall, I heard music playing—I thought "she's having a private party" of some sort.

Later that evening after our kids went to sleep, she lit into me: "Do not *ever* break into the house! If the door is locked, just go away for a while."

"But I *live* here, what's going on?"

It turned out that Jude was hosting a drug deal in our parlor. Three men came to exchange money for a few pounds—*pounds*—of coke and a smaller volume of heroin. The men tested and weighted each drug, cut the volumes into smaller packets and paid the dealer. Like a bizarre Tupperware party, they gave Jude the empty baggies and a small amount of money in exchange for using our home for about two hours . That night we carefully slit open and gently scraped the coke from the inside of its large plastic bag. On the mirror was a big—to us—pile of coke, probably a half gram or more.

I partook of this "windfall" but it spooked me, and fortunately it had scared Jude, too. She did not know these men, they had been referred by another dealer we knew and trusted. But, *heroin*? That brought us close to a level of drug play that I did not want to be involved with. It seemed too out of control, too addictive, too creepy and brought potentially dangerous people into our lives. One of the men had made it plain that he wore a concealed and loaded handgun.

Jude cleaned out the heroin bag and folded up about a quarter gram of the stuff in a square of paper. I wanted nothing to do with it. She was curious about smoking it in a joint. I stayed away. At least *that* time.

Jude swore after that day to do only one more deal in our house. We were taking on another roommate and child—it would mean three to four kids at home most of the time. We could not risk their safety, or ours, by inviting more of this madness into our home.

When I think back on this wild time—and this is the tame, edited version—I shudder to think what our lives could have become if we were caught dealing—or worse, if the men had decided we no longer had a choice in the matter of opening our home to them.

Early in my painting career, I met a couple of women, Tina and Jo, and we teamed up, to share in the work we found. They smoked pot several times per day: A joint after breakfast, a joint after lunch, after work and into the evening. They lived downstairs from a cocaine dealer, and coke became a part of their evening routine; soon, their daytime routine as well. Using became their lifestyle, and when they got too high, they brought out whiskey or wine to come down again.

I quickly learned that I could not work effectively while stoned. If I got high during the day job, I became fuzzy and my efficiency suffered. I didn't relish the idea of falling from scaffolding or a ladder either. I would be too tired to do the night work at the café. And, I did not like coming home to my daughter stoned. Whenever we "partied" with coke and pot, I could not consume as much as everyone else, and could not add alcohol to the mix—I just could not keep up no matter how I tried! Now, of course, I thank god for my genetic makeup or whatever it was that prevented me from taking too much.

Nevertheless, I developed a bit of a coke habit; I wanted it when I didn't have it. I was mildly addicted and loved the feeling of mental "clarity" I thought I felt from the stimulant effect. We used to say: dope will get you through times of no money better than money will get you through times of no dope. My clients sometimes unknowingly paid for my habit. When I bid a painting job for them, I added the cost of a gram of coke to the tab, like adding on ten percent for possible overages. It was a game to me, perhaps more serious to my friends.

Tina and Jo often hired a man who sometimes worked with, sometimes *for* them. Jo had grown up in the same neighborhood as Bobby, and he taught her to paint. But he did not have the communication skills or confidence to get work on his own and his reputation for burning bridges and drinking on the job made him unreliable. So, whenever Tina and Jo did not want to do a certain level of work—the degree of difficulty too high, or greater strength was required, Jo hired Bobby to do it.

During and after work, of course, drugs and beer helped them get through the day. Occasionally, I worked with them. And took drugs with them. One night we all partied together at Tina and Jo's. We chipped in some of our earnings to buy a gram of coke and dinner. We ate, laughed, told stories and "tripped" until the wee hours. I wore out by one a.m. and wanted to go home. Taking more coke was just happening because it was there, it did not get me any higher. Jo got out the bourbon to bring us all down, but not being able to handle liquor, I declined and made ready to go.

Bobby sat in a rocking chair, grinding his teeth, spaced out most of the night. Jo made fun of him and he laughed back but I don't think he actually heard her—there was no light in his eyes, no real recognition. He laughed nervously and said coldly, "c'mon, let's do it!" meaning, let's do the coke until it's gone. I left.

Tina and Jo phoned me about three days later. "Bobby just called to say goodbye. The police are on their way to arrest him." Apparently, he had remembered that he might have killed his landlady a few days ago.

Turns out, the night we all partied together, Bobby had gotten so high, Jo had to escort him to his rooms across the street to make sure he got home all right. Sometime during the early morning hours, still awake and in need of more coke, he climbed up the back deck of the house, broke into his landlady's home and strangled her for the money belt she wore about her waist. With several hundred dollars to spend, he called around to find more drugs. Bobby's cocaine bender lasted two days. He confessed to the murder and was sent to Folsom Prison for fifteen years to life. For all I know, he is still there. He left his estranged wife and five-year old daughter behind to wonder and grieve.

Reality crashed in and all the fun drained out of the drug scene for me. I wanted no part of it. Though it took a while to stop wanting coke, pot seemed easy to quit and I could certainly live with less alcohol. I did not like the person I had become to use drugs. I didn't trust my own judgment and tried very hard to cover my confusion and lack of confidence by moving fast and moving on. I moved to another street.

Even after the experience with Tina, Jo and Bobby, thinking I was done with the drug life, I had a brief fling with "chewie" or crack: washed coke sprinkled into a joint or cigarette and smoked. I thought I was above the people on the street who loved smoking pure crack cocaine in a pipe. I could take it or leave it. But as I played in this field,

I could feel the old druggie stinkin'-thinkin' creeping back in, making me special, wanting to allow drugs into the center of my life again. I quit again.

A short time after I quit using, I began a relationship with a really nice man. He was in alcoholic recovery, and since I had given up the drug scene, I thought it was a really good sign that we were together. After a week he left. Went away and never came back, never called or wrote or acknowledged me in any way, leaving me devastated and confused. The morning he left without saying goodbye, I hopped into my van to get to work and almost immediately became the emergency brake for a woman who was so drunk at nine a.m. that she passed out at the wheel, ran a red light at full speed and nearly cut the van in two.

That night, ignoring my trauma from the wreck, I bought some coke, borrowed a car and drove to Monterrey in search of this man who said we would have a weekend together, but decided to disappear instead. I drove all over Monterrey and Carmel, with no idea where he might be, or even if he was anywhere near there, a mad, desperate attempt to—what? Find love, justice, explanation, hope?

Back in the hood, I fell in with some folks who lived down the street. The same pattern ensued: a bit of weed after work followed by parties with coke and booze; all-nighters with people I ordinarily would steer away from. I realized I was going nowhere again. I accepted an assignment to teach in Alaska for a year—which gave me six months to get *really* sober! Really!

I moved again. I made new friends. My new sober roommate had a child about my daughter's age—it turned out to be a pretty good match. Mel also worked in the trades. We shared our stories and tried in our own ways to work with the wreckage of our lives and become better parents. Mel found Insight Meditation helped him stay sober and keep growing. I attended a meditation school, too, and would not only graduate, but go on to teach in that system for seventeen years.

I worked in the trades off and on for about fifteen years, but quit working with Tina and Jo. Jo, always a bit edgy, became paranoid and a rude loud mouth. As time went on, she became more demanding and irrational, flying into a rage or leaving nasty messages on my answering machine. Eventually, Tina left her. As far as I can tell, Tina mostly left the drugs behind as well. But Jo never did. Today she has a long list of health issues, relies on social security disability, blames the world for her troubles, and is considered to have bi-polar disorder. She's a mess.

Cocaine makes you greedy, plus selfish, and more paranoid—all your precious gift of consciousness goes toward getting more, getting more than your friend got, getting it all the time, getting so high that you can't get higher but you still try. Pot by itself will tend to make people paranoid and cranky, but with coke and alcohol your life can spin out of control in the time it takes to tie your shoelaces.

LSD: been there and done that. Wish I could do it again. But an LSD trip is unpredictable—could be a nice ride and get nicer; could go to hell fast and get worse. You are on a roller coaster and cannot get off until it's done with you.

I had a few mind-opening trips and two that were real nightmares. My friends had all had bad trips, too, though the fun usually outweighed the bad trips.

Tim Leary and Ram Dass and the Beatles had made a whole

generation love the high, the heart and mind opening experiences, and the expanded consciousness of a good acid trip. I'm glad to hear that some therapists are doing real research with acid, Ecstasy and similar mind-altering drugs, because I believe, and have proof in a few friends, of real benefit from controlled and supervised use of these drugs for psychological discoveries and healing.

Leary rode the LSD gravy train most of his adult life; Ram Dass freed himself after a few years. During one of his trips to India, Ram Dass experienced a revelation about drugs. When I first heard him speak of it in 1990, an experience I had already had started to make sense. He talked at length about the fun of being high, feeling a state of love and unity with everyone, the world, and the joy of expanded consciousness that produced those feelings. Then he said, "…but getting high wasn't getting free. And what I wanted was to be free."

I understood that realization, and lived it in the mid 1980s without finding the right words at the time to describe the eventual empty plane of reality following an LSD trip (or a night of cocaine, for that matter). You literally and figuratively "come down" and life inside is not the same. What would I do with all that glorious expanded consciousness? I would cram it back down into a small, spiritually immature inner life, and bore my friends attempting to explain the high thoughts and insights that I could not possibly live. A spiritual depression, to match the biological post-trip low, descends, and whatever existential fears I already harbor, comes crashing back in to exact revenge for my self-abandonment.

Terrified, I want to get up, get high again. Fast. But high is not *free*. And the choice is clear once I discovered there was a choice. I chose to feel free. If I had not felt the truth of freedom, I might have lost all will to remain on the ground and may not be living the immeasurably rich inner life I live today.

Chapter 5: Finding *Courage to Change*

CHILDREN OF ALCOHOLICS HAVE BEEN well trained to be good enablers. Co-dependence describes how we become addicted to the alcoholic. Parents, no matter how harsh, gone, distracted, addicted, or lying, conniving, narcissistic or stupid, kept us alive and we know it. Some have given us just enough kindness to really hook our self-esteem, to addict us to the infrequent morsels of attention and hope they could spare in a given moment. To stand up for ourselves can feel really unsafe, disloyal, dangerous, or even unkind—and sometimes it *seems* to require soul-rending rage for us to create individual breathing room.

My mother was one of the kindest people I have ever known, and she abandoned us all for her alcoholic stupors. She was one of the most interesting, intelligent and well-read women I have ever met, and she offered little guidance or support for our own development. She could be rational, cautious and caring, and she put us at risk many times because she was drinking. She was loving, but not of herself; giving but not *to* herself; seemingly humble, but proud of her ability to have handled people who enabled her addiction and denial; she manipulated people for pity and complicity, and used her sad story as "social currency" to buy power and uphold her rationalizations for drinking and not getting help. She lied.

It seems to me some of the nicest, funniest, most wonderful people in this world are addicts—they have an illness as horrendous as heart disease, diabetes or cancer—and our culture is just beginning to get smarter about the *disease* of alcoholism. Not there yet. Alcoholics are ill and they may be my parents, and I love them, and they are ill. And, they need help that I cannot give them.

I sometimes wonder if I had acted sooner, drawn firm lines and held them, perhaps my mother might have gone sober sooner. But I now know, I am not in control of any other human being, especially an alcoholic.

The stances I could have taken sooner—"call her bluff," refuse to talk on the phone, refuse to allow her to drive, refuse to be drawn into the drama, to get captivated by her incessant talking, to stop offering solutions so she can argue harder for her limitations—are all clearly apparent in retrospect. In Al-Anon we call this "if only" thinking. It can drive you nuts. The only line I drew early on was to tell Mother she could not—ever—drive my children anywhere if she had been drinking. But I did not draw that line for myself until I was much older.

I, and maybe you, *feel the call* to stand up for self and children or grandchildren, stand up for sanity, stand up for the right to live and be happy—and take action accordingly. I must wake myself all the time, and stop allowing the out of control person (in me or another) to control my life. As they used to say, "Not standing up for yourself is like letting the waiter eat your supper."

Taking on the bones...

Xmas morning

Tangerines in our stockings. And nuts. We could always expect tangerines and walnuts in the shell in our stockings. Rarely, chocolate. Occasionally resurrected Halloween candy that had lain in Mother's secret coffee can storage facility for 2 months. Or a year and 2 months.

Mother always provided. She somehow managed to give us pajamas and slippers and sometimes robes for Christmas, along with a toy or two. Often she got us each a big toy—something we really wanted. And a small pile of sensible things, art supplies, socks. One Christmas, I expressed the desire for a bike, a real bike, a two-wheeler, that I could learn to ride in order to keep up with the other kids. Under the tree that Christmas morning was a huge tricycle, used but in fair condition. Embarrassed, I rode it only on the porch, never in the street. The message of this big trike seemed clear to me: too big for your britches.

At Easter we three kids each had new clothes: shoes, hats, dresses, a suit for Billy, and Mother might have a new hat, too. She was clever with sewing and decorating, so I imagine she dyed, re-decorated or re-mixed her wardrobe often so we could afford new things. There were no credit cards then. You could put items on layaway, and she likely did that as well, to acquire our Christmas or Easter stuff.

We were poor. At first, I thought we were just lucky that during the night a case box of different cereals or other foods would magically appear on the front porch. I learned later that the folks at the local grocery took pity on my mother raising three kids on her own. In spite of the fact that she kited checks at this store, some of the employees "damaged" inventory so they could add an item to a box for us.

The crushing indictment of "poor" was confirmed by our Virginia cousins when I was ten—we were the poor relations, poor benighted souls of the lost family of privileged ones, whose inheritance was lost long ago. Fallen aristocracy. I unconsciously allowed that thought to seep from my senses into my bones.

The story told to us was that we carry old family names that everyone should recognize, like Rockefeller, Getty or Luce. The loss of financial power behind our inherited names, coupled with the confusion and tragedy attached to our incarcerated, mentally ill father, seemed to signify our name rhymed with shame.

As Mother would say: pillar to post, hand to mouth—that's how we lived. True or not that is how I *believe* I have lived. I *wish* to have it easier but find the perceptual habit of living 'hand to mouth' is hard to break. It comprises the default frame around my financial picture and social prospects. Poor. Gobs of potential, but tragic—the old indictments leveled against Mother seemed to stain my record before I was given a chance to make my own.

I have taken apart many old traumas, and feel much stronger in myself because of it. But this poverty is a damning conclusion of mind, an expectation felt in the heart as the shame percolates up from a stomach already soured with money worry. My expectations for life, sunk low, became blighted by the cold light of reality of what I "don't got" in evidence. So many sweet dreams and worthy desires starved at the root for lack of encouragement and faith.

What I dreamt for—education, career, travel, solid marriage—meant a huge departure from the path laid out by my childhood. I began to scale my desires back before they took free expression, confining the struggling seedlings of desire to tiny pots and holding them back until their imprisoned roots strangled my hopes from underground.

I couldn't seem to commit to the ground of my being where roots could spread—no, I did not trust myself or providence to nurture them. So many little plans in rigid pots, holding, waiting, dying in confinement. My garden, my life, my soul—who might I have become, what might I have done if I had found room to breathe, soil to dig deeply into, sky and water—precious light and space to stretch and grow?

Writing about poverty, I can feel the taboo arise: don't go there, shameful. Don't explore it, don't reinforce the beliefs. Well, I disagree. I want to release poverty of spirit from my self-concept; I want my record expunged and sealed, done with. And I will assist myself by writing it aright and out of my body and mind.

I dream that my sister, brother and I have moved to a rural location. I have no money and need to pay rent or buy food or something. "Would it be worth something to you for me to get rid of this?" I ask my siblings, meaning the bones and evidence of vermin all over this house. Appearances are very important. Next scene, I'm burying the bones in a bog-like depression in the earth. I come back later and do it again to make sure it is well done.

This dream hints at a bargain struck in early life, an unconscious agreement to take on the bones, dispose of the shadows, and bury them deep within me, in exchange for my belonging and survival in the family. Where is this bog-like depression? A watery marsh in my psyche? A water element organ within my body?

Even in my dreams I can sometimes feel the shame of poor-ness. Not real or grinding poverty, of course, but what I felt and could sense from Mother—*not enough.* Fear that no matter what the challenge I am not enough, do not have enough, to thrive. I live in pretty nice quarters, have good work to do, but I live with my nose just above water.

A dream fragment where I am shopping for shoes and feeling the pressure of time and of others waiting for me.

There is a weary sadness and dis-comfort with money, with shopping. A fear that spending on *this* might mean I don't have money for *that*. Spending sacrifices the presumed safety of having a 'bird in hand'. Always wrestling in my mind about the wisdom of buying anything—a pair of shoes is going to take from the rent or food allowance. Any purchase for self is frivolous, foolish, no matter if it is necessary. There isn't enough for me, for what I want, ever. I am stuck with a used tricycle.

Another dream fragment: Mother and me in a café. I say to the writers sitting near us, working in their craft: "I don't know how you guys do it, write fiction. I can tell you a story but not in writing. I can't write a novel."

I know the principle that we create our own reality and "all stories are psycho-diagnostic," so that little snippet of facing my mother-myself and saying I don't know how you guys make up stories, provokes me. Considering the three dreams together, this last dream seems to suggest that I hold a belief that I don't know how you make up a *different* story—another reality. And I don't understand how three kids growing up with the same mother, can have radically different expectations for themselves in life. How do I write myself into a better life story?

To write a new story also calls into question the one I've been living to get to this point. And, if it's so easy—just make up a new story and jump into it—kinda makes me look a little foolish for hanging around and suffering all these years, doesn't it?

Before I knew anything about myself, I took on the old energy, the bones and vermin of family history, and buried them so no one knows. I don't know how to write myself a new story, without exhuming the old one, to form a new agreement to enable another life. My story, which feels like Mother's, reeks of guilt, shame and monumental doubt about my value in this life.

Taking on the bones has meant accepting the legacy, the weight of Mother's depression—the era of the Great Depression, the loss of family dignity, social status and entitlement, in exchange for acceptance—and I'm still at it. Maybe we kids all took it on—the depression/The Depression—the loss of family face and name significance in the world.

I used to think my Virginia cousins didn't appear to be so burdened with shame about or around money and lifestyle. My brother and sister seemed to me to have escaped the pressure of the family past. But I know better now—none of us escaped unscathed by our family history and alcoholism. Maybe those early perceptions have been my *fiction*, my novel I read so deeply and intently, that I can't see that I'm also writing it!

Now, however I *am* writing a new story for myself. Every time I turn over the old one and make new discoveries, I seem to move off that square and on to a blank one. I fill the new square with new meaning, new permission, a sense of rightness, fiction or no. I'll write down these bones in recognition for my life now. Writing Mother's story, writing down *them* bones, will be my last great debt payment to family. The faster I let go of that old story, write it out, the faster I get to develop my own. I make room for all my new self-images by *dis*-containing the old ones.

And so, I give myself permission to write out all that my mother gave to me for safe-keeping, such as her fear, like mine, of the criticism of others. She, too, felt trapped in an agreement with her family of origin. She carried *her* mother's pain and shame in her body and life, too. To lay that story aside feels disloyal in the extreme, as if severing from the legacy severs us from the *source* of life—our mother's milk, however strained and tainted that nourishment had become.

I'm more dedicated now to tell their stories because my life appears to depend upon it! I need to write them down, and out, because they are *stories*. I need for myself to now make the distinction that these stories are past and gone, because until now I didn't and haven't. I took them in as truth, the truth of my inheritance.

I am learning by doing—by applying principles I learned outside the family system. Thus, that old saying that family teaches survival but not evolution, has finally found, or hit, home in me.

"Take my advice, I'm not using it right now..."

What I have learned:

The following are examples of what I have learned, especially in Al-Anon, and am still learning, since I began to really examine my life. These "points" come from my real life experiences and others' stories, and the places inside where these ideas have helped me to grow. I hope you will find something helpful, something hopeful, to take along with you for your own evolution—

- **The alcoholic/addict MUST seek his/her own help.**

Family cannot play the role of therapist-helper. Family *can* set reasonable boundaries with firm compassion (what used to be called "tough love") and can arrange for professional intervention to alert the parent or family member to the end of denial and enabling within the family system.

I may have helped my mother come to realize some aspect of her drinking problem, but I believe it was a *confluence* of realizations from *multiple sources* that finally helped her admit she had a problem.

- **Family members should seek help whether the alcoholic does or not.**

Children of Alcoholics, or COAs, are especially vulnerable because we, too, are hooked—I got hooked on helping, hooked on hating, feeling sad, hopeful, helpless, damaged, shamed, vengeful and powerless. I got hooked being the child of an alcoholic!

I am in a life-long re-learning process in how to stand for myself, for health, for change, for truth and transparency. I need to see my *own* denial and develop healthier outlets for my stress and frustration and more genuine expressions for my feelings. My addicted parents couldn't help *me* find this sort of help, just as I cannot help them. You know the old saw: don't jump in to save a drowning person if you don't know how to swim.

- **AA and Al-Anon are powerful bridges to sobriety for many people.**

Sober alcoholics help recovering alcoholics; recovering Adult Children of Alcoholics help other ACAs. And, qualified therapists, knowledgeable of Alcoholism, have also helped me come back to my senses from the deeply light-deprived, dishonest, depressive and oppressive environment of my dysfunctional family.

- **I have to work it inside to see it outside:** I can't allow the outer condition to control my serenity, my sense of self, or my future.

To say *circumstances* is to point to the ideas, beliefs and attitudes I was standing in that helped to create what I see in my life today. The word literally suggests a circle around where I am standing. So if I don't like what I think I see, I need to determine to learn something about the *me* that helped to create *this*. I need to assess my*self*, more than what the outer situation appears to be. Self-assessment is not blame; it is how I come to recognize where I am in life and how I got there; it is how I make corrections in my thinking and being in order to create something else.

If you grew up in a dysfunctional or addicted family, you likely became accustomed to running your life from the outside in. Addiction and alcoholism, and all its' many subtle and not so subtle ways of insuring its own survival and centrality in *my* life, was daily present— it was my custom, my dictum, my religion, my focus. Alcohol was smarter and more determined than I was.

Recovery and serenity seems more possible for me when I gently take back the authority I have given to addiction and to the addicted, and focus on myself. The activity most damaging and undermining to addiction and co-dependency is turning attention to my own inner life. Honesty, transparency, and a quiet determination to show up for myself, brings healing light to my situation, acceptance to my self-concept. The honesty fosters compassion in all my relationships, beginning with me.

Meditation and *Focusing* are the methods by which I turn and listen to my insides, shutting out the outside influences, and even quieting or quelling the part of me that is most often run by the outside or other people.

- **I am like the alcoholic:**

My negative self-talk is the alcoholic's denial cleverly turned inward:

The alcoholic is still drinking in me, drinking me in. Self-talk and obsessing are my ways of talking to the alcoholics of my life: convincing, cajoling, punishing, defending, judging, fixing, being right, having the last word; and being damned arrogant, dramatic, hateful and self-sympathizing-without-compassion-for-self-or-others about it. All learned behaviors that I am slowly un-learning and replacing with kinder ways of being.

- **Posture:**

As in *posturing*, taking a stand for an illusion or lie.

Sometimes I posture, because I am too sure, and I need to plumb my reasoning to catch denial, naiveté, defensiveness and my determination to be the opposite of my alcoholic qualifiers.

Sometimes it means a literal, *physical* posture, because that is what I saw. One day I filled my class with water, looked out the window and began to drink. Something in my posture got my attention—my pelvis was thrust forward a little, left hand on hip, right tilting the glass, and an odd tension in my neck. I stopped mid-swallow to feel into my body. This was unlike me, unlike my way of standing. Then, I *sense*-remembered: this is the way my mother stands at the sink as she drinks vodka and water. See Chapter 1, "Across the street from my childhood."

- **Assumptions:** The old saying goes—to assume makes an *ass* of *u* and *me*

Note to self: Do not Assume the addicted person is telling the truth. *Grow up!*

- **Attitude:** Question the *Authority* of an Attitude, my condemnation prior to investigation; a defense in advance of the assumed outcome.

My mother's attitude about her woes: I am too intelligent for any psychologist to help; I can't be helped; there is no help for my pain.

Of course, her attitude kept her from *seeking* help. To seek help would mean admitting to a problem. To admit that she had failed at managing her relationship with alcohol would also mean, for Mother, that she could no longer hide behind her sensitivity and her faulty thinking. Alcoholic addiction ran the show. She would have to face the fact that she had used her sad life events as a reason to drink, and used drink as a means of controlling all aspects of her life; that she lied to herself and others about her predicament; that alcohol was in charge of her health, wealth and happiness—that she had a *disease* called Alcoholism.

My attitude was: I don't need Al-Anon or recovery groups; I know how to meditate and I do energy healing on myself. I can take care of it. This was the way I continued to hide out and pretend I knew more than others about addiction and its effects on my inner life.

- **Character:** Honesty and Transparency

The biggest character flaw in alcoholics is called out into the open with Step 1 from Alcoholics Anonymous: *Admitted we were powerless over alcohol.*

The biggest character flaw in the sober friends and family of alcoholics is 'outed' in the same way: *Admitted we were powerless over alcohol* and the alcoholic, and the disease of alcoholism, or the dysfunction in the family. In the same way the alcoholic allows the substance to be their primary relationship, run their lives, and control time, money, intimacy, honesty and faith, so I have made the alcoholic (or dysfunction) central to my life: helping, fixing, avoiding, defending and hiding my shame in the family system have become my central endeavors. And, unconsciously conducting my relationships with others as I learned to do from observing the alcoholic relating to alcohol.

- **I have to *find* the *courage* to take better care of myself:**

The following are things I have tried and do. It all helps a little and all the little helps add up over time to enable the creation of a more awakened, softened life.

Daily Practices imperfectly performed:

:: Learn more about the motivations behind my own behaviors.

:: Be patient: appreciate what my experience has to teach me. Healing is not as dramatic as ripping out circuits and stomping out of the room.

:: Slow my expectations for *relief*. Face my need for *rescue*.

:: Practice tolerance for **myself** in my process; admit my vulnerability.

:: Determine and seek to come into a different relationship with my life   and challenges rather than wasting precious time and energy trying to fix it "out there.

- **Amends**

I have been harmed, I have harmed another and myself through thought, words or actions. There is an energy signature left over: betrayal, anger, sadness, worry, shame. Various practices suggest I try writing letters to make amends, or to begin the process of learning how to make amends. (Al-Anon sponsors can join you in role-playing to make amends, too.) These letters I write are less about apology, more about behaviors, realizations and my personal commitment to amend the behavior. I do not send them until they have incubated for a week or two. I must not be in a hurry! And, I may decide to re-write or scrap it all together.

Also, I learned my injured party need not be present to receive my amends. And, I need not be present to receive amends from another. One man I had been involved with turned out to be addicted to crack cocaine. Mood swings and violence and dangerous rows were always waiting in the wings. I walked on egg shells around him. About six months after we parted, he began to call and pester me about his need to make amends to me for his behaviors. I did not want to engage with him at all. I consulted with Rose, an AA friend of mine, and she reminded me that I did not have to be present for him to make amends! His pestering was an attempt to get into my life in some way and I should not take the bait. I listened to a tape by Marianne Williamson, describing how to leave a relationship like mine, and I decided to borrow some of her words. I called this man's voice mail and left the following message: "Make your amends with your sponsor. You are a liar, a cheat and a scoundrel, and I love you, and I want nothing more to do with you. Do not call me again." And he didn't.

Regarding letter writing: Julia Cameron says, writing it down is writing it *out*. Out of the mind, out of my body, out of my life.

Here is a practical idea from Colin Tipping's *Radical Forgiveness* book and training. I have used this process many times and taught it to others. It can be a very powerful shifter for attitudes and feelings, especially when I am the injured party.

Colin Tipping's method: Write three letters—to the alcoholic offender, to god, to the universe, the family, myself or whomever. By hand, on paper. **Note: I will not mail these letters!**

The first letter: let it all hang out! All the rage, sadness, grief, guilt or shame I have been harboring. Let that letter be nasty, biting and outrageous, but also specific. Let every grievance be known and written down. **I do not mail this letter!**

The second letter: An hour or a day later, write the second letter. Again, I allow my feelings to come out onto the paper. I explore the specifics of how I think I was injured, my perspective and what this event has come to mean in my life. I notice that some of the high emotional charge has died down a little, and some clearer ideas and values have begun to work their way into my words.

I do not mail this letter!

The third letter: A few hours or a day later, write the third letter. This letter may explore the event one more time. This time, I allow other *possible explanations* to come forward, not to excuse me or the other from our respective parts in the situation, but to explore other possibilities for what this scenario may come to mean to me, how I will store it in memory.

I do not mail this letter

Tipping says this kind of processing leads to taking responsibility for your part, and for creating the opportunity to adopt a different view to challenge the habit of dwelling in pain or anger. He also encourages us to seek a positive viewpoint as a powerful first step to creating a radical forgiveness habit. He says: look at the circumstance or situation and deliberately seek a positive viewpoint, declaring:

- Look what I have created (or co-created).

- Somehow, on a level I cannot yet see, this situation is perfect.

- I am ready to begin to glimpse the perfection in this situation.

Then, I let it go. I refuse to dwell. Instead, I allow the powerful wisdom of nature to deliver, through insight and intuition, the real truth of the situation, the truth that will truly set me free. This whole process—writing the three letters, acknowledging what I have created and being willing to glimpse the perfection—has opened up my life and perspective, not just when I am at odds with someone. Working inside this way has helped me prepare for true forgiveness.

- **Expand: realizing my world has gotten smaller**

When I am triggered, I crawl into a small part inside, a hurt part. My perspective is shrunken down to what I can see in order to survive. Expanding helps to open me up again. It is not a way to ignore my hurt, or go unconscious. Expanding gives me time. Time to get into my hobbies, have fun, dance, sing, meet new people, take a vacation, go to concerts, take a walk, read, invest in myself and my future, get help and counseling, join a group with a community project or political focus. Take myself on an artist date, or creator/powerful person (ala Julia Cameron) dates! Go learn something new. Speak up, speak out, honor my own voice and perspective. In other words, MOVE!

- **Appreciate Beauty: inside and out**

I now have many beauty "touch-stones" in my life, my inner life: noticing beauty in the world is a symptom of beauty stirring in me. I try to notice and collect beauty often. I select a small object or word that sums up, for now, the beauty I feel growing within me. I carry that object or word with me. I touch it often to remind myself I am building a beautiful sense of aliveness within.

- **Make a Separation: I am not you**

I had to learn to see myself as autonomous, separate from the other (alcoholic or crazy person) and his reality. Careful, open, embodied listening to myself helps me to know I have my own reality to reflect upon, to really see, sense and feel my own experience. And, I am enough. Knowing all that, I am a better listener for others.

- **Focusing**

Focusing is a well-researched, easy to learn practice for identifying and expressing the *felt-sense* of self and experience, and for expanding awareness. Focusing is a natural capacity of consciousness, a way toward positive acceptance and appropriate self-interest.

The practice also allows me to find "right distance" from my pain, my memories and perceptions.

"The actual process of focusing, experienced from the inside, is fluid and open, allowing great room for individual differences and ways of working."

The Focusing Institute

- **SOS or Seek Outside Solutions**

Al-Anon: I can't tell you how powerful it is to be in a room with other people from all walks of life, and to hear how others have lived what I lived and seen what I have seen and suffered like I have suffered in an alcoholic household. No one will give me advice. I will be *heard*. Period. I am accepted, my *experience is accepted*. Period.

Seeking outside solutions creates an environment within me that allows me to be transparent, open and available, versus hiding in shame and not feeling as if I deserve to get help for my problems. SOS takes me *outside* the family's dysfunctional, closed system, where there is no light or fresh air, to share my dilemma with another, to invite a different point of view. Al-Anon, therapy and recovery groups for women are some of the ways I seek outside solutions.

If you feel inspired to do so, visit an Al-Anon group near you. They are easy to find, Google, and often hold meetings in local churches (and on Zoom) every day of the week. See "Getting Clear" for Al-Anon stories and observations.

- **Volunteer:**

Lots of organizations in all communities need volunteer help. Helping others can be a wonderful outlet for that need to be useful! Giving time and caring to others not related to me has also helped me "right size" and "right direct" my energies.

Check out MADD, Mothers Against Drunk Driving (*www.madd.org*). "MADD has helped to save more than 350,000 lives, reduce drunk driving deaths by more than 50 percent and promote designating a non-drinking driver. ...24-Hour Victim Help Line 1-877-MADD-HELP." Visit www.madd.org or call 1-877-ASK-MADD.

PART III

Resources for living with Alcoholism

Chapter 6: Al-Anon and getting clear

In one of his early books, Scott Peck talked about how we learn from the dysfunction we live within. Paraphrasing: **children learn to conduct relationships from observing their parents' relationship to their addictive substance.** *They say the truth will set you free, but the day I read Peck's words, the truth made me snap the book closed and hurl it across the room. It would be a few more years before I could put that truth to good use in my life.*

Some sobering thoughts about *Sobering Thoughts*:

When I first came to Al-anon and open AA meetings, what I thought I saw and heard stirred a deeply shameful memory. I realize now I equated people humbling themselves in meetings, to what I thought I saw in my mother when she went to worship. My mother seemed to lose 3 or 4 inches in height when she "darkened the doorway" of my childhood church. She seemed bent in shame, defeated, brought low, to the lowest nothing of submission: a sinner, a "not worthy so much as to gather up the crumbs under thy table" kind of lowly scum. She often wept in church, mourning her lost way and yearning for the love of the savior, but never came as equal to the communion table.

I hated seeing her that way, crushed by shame and guilt. Thirty or so years ago, AA and Al-anon members looked that way to me—mindless, spineless, begging for mercy, all dignity gone under the boot of the mean, spiteful, jealous Old Testament God.

At the time, I also believed I had developed sufficient healing power through meditation and energy work to help me overcome any defects of character I had developed or had been infected with in my family. My damaged life skill toolbox was being rapidly re-filled with character building material. I believed family tools for thriving, either broken or missing or twisted out of shape by generations of alcoholism, were being mended by clever words and the grace of a loving, forgiving and helpful *inner* god.

My mother's capital G god could never be given enough: praise, groveling, supplication, power, admission of sin and sheer lowliness compared to Him. It sounded like the ultimate slave-master relationship. And, *He*, seemingly, never really helped my mother. After church the god of alcohol showed her who was her *true* master—she always needed a large, potent dose, to steady her nerves and raise her blood sugar after all that aerobic groveling.

Her humility before her God was humiliating to me.

How dare the church and the prayers I was beginning to actually listen to, be anything but a loving, welcoming, forgiving and guiding model—Jesus promoting gentle spiritual growth. The New Testament seemed to offer a "come as you are and be healed" party; the Old Testament seemed like "come and be dominated" by the sado-masochism of your sins and faults.

My religion became to study people with real, solid character: writers and speakers and successful rich people. I filled my life toolbox with pithy slogans from folks more accomplished than me. I made their words more important than my own, their thoughts more enlightened than mine, and bent my thinking and self-concept toward the living rectitude of better people.

Blinded by light or darkness is still blind.

In AA and Al-anon, the fourth step to living sobriety says, "made a searching and fearless, moral inventory…" My first *scathing and fearful* more or less inventory included a realization about faulty motivations behind my actions and decisions. I am clever. No doubt about it. Clever. Anyone can be clever because of the principle that says, "What we consistently give attention to, develops." I have developed or grown a clever mouth-mind. Like an appendage grown from a twisted frame, *clever* is also a weapon the wounded use to exact revenge. Sometimes I want to wash my mouth out with the same acid that produced my thinly veiled, snarky one-upmanship in the first place.

Re-reading the Twelve Steps I see again—because I have to be shown again—that the given gift of gab has been honed in me like a fine knife—used to cut, to prick the "pricks" and power-hungry people who appear to have hurt me. In her teaching, Maya Angelou used an African expression, "blow, bite and blow" to describe such careful wit—one who 'blows' to anesthetize its adversary with politeness, nips, then blows softly again to make the person doubt they have been bitten. I learned from the masters in my family: set up the naïve to think they matter to you; dress your power in fake benevolence; bite at the heart left undefended; quickly abandon the stunned, leave them feeling duped and responsible at the same time. Clever. You have to be real clever to pull it off.

My clever is also kinder and gentler. My clever is seductive, impressive and flattering. It lets you know how clever I am. It makes you think I am all into *you*, when I am showing off my tendency to obscure my fear and pain.

My *fearful more or less inventory* also includes seeing behind my faulty agendas to my fear of being manipulated by others. This fear has caused me to resent others *in advance*, being sure they are out to disable me. It is deeply ego-offensive to feel weak, gullible and defenseless against smarter people—con men and women. So I learned offensive defensive tactics—barriers of humor and smug refusal to play along, backbiting and getting even in my head.

A rule of thumb in this business is to notice I have been infected by what I see in others—this is both good and bad news. The highly developed traits I admire in others are also available in me, perhaps in seed or budding form. And, the highly developed negative traits, the flaws I see so clearly in others, lay as potentials in me. In an alcoholic family, the crazy-makers would have no power at all if children of alcoholics did not also possess a matching crazy-making component in our own psyches.

As I experienced and learned to fear manipulation in my family, I see now that I also manipulate—I want you to think well of me. I want you to be impressed by how clever and smart I am. Secretly, I want to feel justified in my resentment while hiding my fear in a cloud of knowing. I can get really clever with words and ideas and barrel over yours, out-pun puns, out-perform your expectations, work hard and study and borrow ideas from other smart people to help you do your work on yourself, while I think I'm doing mine by teaching you! It's no wonder I feel like a fraud.

Again, my family imprints are deep, and my coping strategies have been given much latitude in my life. Now I see my responsibility must be to healthy self-assessment, transparency, growing inwardly, and challenging my feelings of inequality within the human family.

My old game requires too much life force energy to keep it going. It is falling apart, and needs to.

Lately I sense all my higher motivations for *Sobering Thoughts* falling from the sky like smog-choked angels. Perhaps they need to do just that. Fall to the ground of reality if they are ever to have impact without pity-seeking. An important ingredient, especially where *ST* is concerned, is *temperance*, with all due irony. Without temperance my well-reasoned and pointed stories in this memoir sound self-pitying, a victim-gone-sour stance. Without temperance and sobriety my stories are diatribe, one harsh indictment after another. How many must I tell to prove the effect, and to voice the *affect*, of my early life in an alcoholism-centered family?

For the sake of *Sobering Thoughts*, I am learning to let these revelations settle in me, rather than mask or avoid them. We never really get rid of anything, least of all our early coping strategies. But I can *change my relationship* to those flaws and learn new and more appropriate strategies for living and thriving. In the language of Al-Anon, it means to *turn it over* and *give it up* for guidance. A bigger, defter hand than mine needs to guide here; to help form the words and ideas that need to come *through* me that will have, I pray, the *sacred* effect of being a positive influence in the world.

My job is not to aspire to perform a sacred act of service, it is to open to the highest and best potential that can come *through* me, without attachment or expectation laced with the needs of my ego-wounded self. I can't do this project justice while keeping a hidden agenda from myself. I should know better than to invite my higher power to tea and try to sell her the Brooklyn Bridge.

So, is *Sobering Thoughts* writing me while I pretend to write *it*?

I set out with a vision that I did not really believe I could pull off—too big for my britches. Again. The temptation to hurry up and write the thing, get it out there and let it help somebody already is a strange urgency borne of a bent sense of duty to manifest my inspiration in form, *right now*. The idea came to *me*, therefore, I should produce it (control it, push it, manipulate with it). Like many ACAs my sense of proportion, perspective and the inner permission I feel are often skewed by two opposing paradigms: delusions of grandeur and an appalling lack of self-esteem. I would not know *balance* if it hit me in the face; couldn't find the middle path with four hands and a flashlight.

Rushing a project such as this is me getting ahead of myself, or trying to control the process of *becoming* the person who could make this book, and all the good intentions that go into it, be worthy of the task of doing service in the world. Like that old, modern cliché: the oxygen mask has to save me first before I attempt to help anyone else.

So I am come back to Al-anon anew: humbled, but not humiliated, exposing my rashness, my cover-ups, my flawed thinking to a room full of folks who, like me, are reaching for healthy self-understanding. I feel relieved in my newly rediscovered transparency, happier and stronger with my more honest assessments, and a newly found respect for emotions being allowed to flow.

"The cure for loneliness is solitude."

—Marianne Moore

According to Tony's A's list, many adult children of alcoholics can:

- Become isolated
- Fear people and authority figures
- Become approval seekers
- Be frightened of angry people
- Be terrified of personal criticism
- Become alcoholics, marry them, or both
- View life as a victim
- Have an overwhelming sense of responsibility
- Be concerned more with others than themselves
- Feel guilty when they stand up for themselves
- Become addicted to excitement
- Confuse love and pity
- "Love" people who need rescuing
- Stuff their feelings
- Lose the ability to feel
- Have low self-esteem
- Judge themselves harshly
- Become terrified of abandonment
- Do anything to hold on to a relationship
- Become "para-alcoholics," people who take on the characteristics of the disease without drinking
- Become reactors instead of actors

I am every one of these. I have employed every one of these as "strategies." I still do, but perhaps less than I have at other times in my life. Determined and appropriate self-interest, meditation, Focusing, time, and perhaps finally outgrowing these old, useless strategies have helped me to grow into being a more available, honest, transparent, loving, growing and creative human being.

Al-Anon

Welcome to the Rooms of Pain and Redemption. To enter is to deliberately open a crypt full of wondrous and monstrous memories, haunting prospects and questionable behaviors. Enter with respect and humbleness for what you see here, what you hear here and for what it may be possible to feel while here. And remember: whom you see here, and what you hear here, are left here, in these rooms, per Anonymity.

Part of what I am encouraged to do is to tell stories, lay out the pain, as it is, as I see it. I do not expect and do not receive any but the barest acknowledgement for spilling my guts onto the floors of these rooms. I might see a few smiles while I spew, might notice a few heads bobbing up and down in recognition, sense the chill of my emotion move round the room and back to me, or feel the invisible support and compassion warm the room beginning with me. But there is no "crosstalk" and no one will question me or call me out. No one will reflect my words to me, though they will listen.

I try to see things, and say things, as they **are**, when I'm in these rooms, because outside these rooms, in the homes and offices and anywhere a relationship with an alcoholic may occur, I lie. I lie to myself, to the other, to the world about the very thing I see, feel, hear, and touch with my life.

To see things as they are, the raging lion, thorn set deeply in the paw, pain out of all proportion, I might rightly conclude all alcoholics are raging, violent. Not to say all alcoholics throw tantrums or beat their spouses or terrify their children. Yet all alcoholics engage with a form of violence that anneals the psyche to a pattern of deep shame and rage that only distilled spirits can dull. To live in denial is to do violence to the peace and truth-loving beings I know we all are; to drink in denial is to seek to dully, and ever so slowly, poison the part of one's awareness that *knows* we are, at base, peace and truth-loving beings.

I seek to see things as they are, and dignity for what it is: Often the last shred of self-respect, the final veil threatening to drop before I am utterly naked, vulnerable and crushable under the weight of daylight. Dignity is not pride, for often in these situations, pride is hubris, pride is demented. No, dignity says, "Tuck in your shirt, smooth back your hair before you move out into the light." Dignity is not just a show of face, it is a need to show that if I have two wits together, I can re-capture the rest of my wits, I will make it and will not be available for a pity party.

In these rooms I reach to see things as they are, though I long for what cannot be. I may never again be casually unconscious in relationship; I can never assume I know the truth of the situation even though I think I do; I cannot take any easy period for granted; I can never, ever assume to have control over anything or anybody. I can no longer, again, trust as I may have thought I did when I was a child. Trust will not come easily, nor be tempted to stay in place, guiding my experience. Trust will be hard to come by, hard to re-learn, re-build, or re-awaken in me. I will learn the hardest lesson about trust, the lesson that will forever close the door on my naive past: that I am the only one truly deserving of my trust. And to be strong and thrive, for self-trust to see me through all the roads ahead, I will need to earn it every day by proving my *trustworthiness* to myself.

It is often said that *pain is weakness leaving the body*; I believe that about denial, that pain is denial leaving the body. To live the life of a co-dependent or adult child of an Alcoholic is to live in pain, recount pain, testify to pain. In testifying I re-experience some of the pain, mostly as grief. There is sometimes unbearable sadness when having to be in these rooms, listening to and telling these tales, trying to figure out how I got into this predicament in the first place. And learning. I open myself to be educated by the Twelve Steps, the realities behind those steps and why I give them attention and time in my lives.

Some folks really work the steps, take their inventories, bare their souls to their sponsors and grow, painfully grow one hard step at a time. Others take the steps in and consider them, let them quietly take root in the psyche until they are ready to see and sense how they play out in a life. I sometimes have a "step sister" in my life, a woman (or a group of women) with whom I can reflect on the steps one at a time. At this writing, I vacillate on the need for another sponsor, a person to whom I will be accountable, and who may have a deeper understanding, and therefore desire, to walk me along the straight and narrow path of co-recovery.

I see my path through Al-Anon as a path to awareness, not specifically to each step, but to a broader and deeper understanding of what I live everyday: I am the child of an alcoholic and am drawn to people with addictions. I have discovered very few actual addictions within me—principally adrenaline—letting fear run my life. But I have one glaring addiction that needs my attention if I am to remain awake and aware in my life: I am addicted to the alcoholic, to fixing the addict him or herself.

I can become swirled into a closed system of communication, hiding, blaming and shaming and avoiding truth. My recovery is about regaining my center, my sense of self first as a damaged child and traumatized adult and second as a smart person who has capacities she often forgets to use, capacities that are returning and redeveloping within her.

I am still capable of learning new things, new ways of being. My body is able to build muscles and change its posture and to enhance its aliveness through movement. My mind likes movement as well, and functions best when curious, awake and open. I am finding a voice again—for singing, and also for writing and immediate conversation. The practice of Focusing has been good training in re-entering the world of my body and re-learning its languages of feeling, sense and imagery. The best use of my mind is to be the servant to the sense of self that *is*, and that is also becoming.

I am powerless over so much, my belly gets hard thinking about it. I read about a woman who said she was playing with the "Let go, let God" mantra with her breath, and realized it had shifted to *Let God let go* within her. It was a happy moment for her, and I got it, the discovery of a simple tool to get you through a big hairy passage. Let God let go, for me. Let God take the very thing that I am wrestling with and let go of it—which combines "give it up" and "let go" all in the same mantra. I am going to try it. Now.

If it is true we are not just dreaming when asleep, but always dreaming, every moment of the day, then I want to know more about, pay better attention to, the way I capture myself, my spirit and senses, within the dream of life I am dreaming. How is it that I live in a state of dreaming all day and night, call one "reality" and the other "sleep?". Dream Implant: Imagine what kind of life I might lead if I liked myself more, if my defaults were compassion and forgiveness.

I'm putting it all into practice, one failure at a time.

Al-Anon Meetings I attend are a form of intimacy with strangers. We get to know one another, we hug and welcome each other. But we are not friends or lovers or family in the room, though some members like to call the folks in the room "family" or "my family." I know why they do this. It is to alleviate the pain of being orphaned in my own real family, and who wants to associate with them anyway after what I've been through? The first time I heard someone include me as "family" I flinched. For a while I felt I had a kind of tic when I heard it because *family* spelled dysfunction, abandonment and pain to me. I am more used to hearing it now.

In these rooms I can share bits of my life and process with honesty and transparency, mostly. It is a form of self-assessment that requires only one listener and no comments, cross talk or back talk. This form of witnessing generates patience in the speaker and in the listener—in either role I am building tolerance for hearing about my/our pain, breakthroughs, mistakes, again, and the small triumphs. In these rooms recognition and compassion help promote self-acceptance. No one comments on my "share" after I speak, though after the meeting adjourns I may hear a bit of it come back to me in compliment form, appreciation for my words that impacted or spoke to or for another. In that way, Al-Anon is a healthier family and home than I have ever experienced before.

The Fires

On the morning of October 9, 2017, fire that began in Napa County as small wild fires, crossed a ridge into Sonoma County and fragmented, if you can use such a word to describe a fire breaking apart and jumping ahead of itself, to the right and left, while it roared down the mountains into Santa Rosa. In Santa Rosa 43 people were taken so unaware, they perished before the Fire Department was fully aware of the nature of these fires, or could respond. Most of the response was simply to get people out of their beds and out into a car or something to convey them to safety. There was no time to turn on a fire hose in those early hours. Just evacuate.

Parts of Santa Rosa, the Coffey Park neighborhood, the Journey's End mobile home park, acres of buildings, and some five thousand homes were burned completely. Some stores and restaurants burned to the ground; Trader Joe's roof caved in; Paradise Ridge Winery reduced to a shell of its former self; the Round Barn in the Fountain Grove area, gone utterly. Big hillsides of homes in the Mark West Springs area, gone. The fire was fickle: it jumped over homes and roads, hit a home here and there, moved in and out of woodland areas, hopscotched over fields and marched down valleys.

Nearly 9000 homes, businesses and other structures were lost in and around Sonoma County. They have now stopped searching for a few "MIAs" amid the ashes.

One thing I know about these fires: There will be a marathon of recovery scenarios, rebuilding and re-settling thousands of lives anew. There is no short run to solutions, cleanup and disposal of the ashes and the toxic ground materials any more than there is an immediate answer to the loss of life, homes, businesses, or way of life that changed utterly in an instant.

People perished in the fires, along with their car keys, or whatever it was they were searching for when the fire and smoke overcame them. Some died in their beds, the fire sealing them within the coverlets, pulling them down into the earth, reducing them to duff in short order. Many thousands of us watched in helpless horror. Those who were not immediately affected, who hung back, beached on their couches, watching their TVs, desperate to help as they were to avoid, stymied by indecision and overwhelming need to respond to the cause, could only turn inward to their own families and friends in helplessness and confused longing.

I felt an impact like "many souls trying to get your divine attention" as Catherine Ponder once put it. There is a call to arms in the community—come help the healing, bend your life in the direction of other people's suffering. But how does one go to help, when helping has been the bane of relationship with others for so long—over sharing, over helping, taking responsibility, inserting oneself into another's life to avoid one's own. Though I live far enough from the fires, I feel the impact: the loss of people, loss of continuity and the norm. These losses in my community are personal losses multiplied. I want to share the load. I wait to hear from the heavens or have delivered in the mail or on my doorstep, the exact right steps I can take to be of help. All I can think to do is to give food and blood. The parallels between the fires and co-dependency stirs the pot and increases the pressure to be productive, a doer, a healer, fixer or helper.

Any trauma, great or small, can light up the entire string of old traumas in a life. Trauma re-traumatizes. In the same way zombies are re-animated humans and seek flesh, old traumas run amok inside like packs of wild dogs on the prowl for any situation wherein they might gain vent to their wildness, their blood lust.

Re-traumatizing in me lights a fire with a strange speed and necessity, like the one that flew down the mountains east of Santa Rosa, and in a flash, ignited whole neighborhoods. My adrenal fires run me around like an excited chicken, squawking and spewing commentary, head removed.

Re-traumatized, because stress is already compounded within and makes me want to compound it without, take any small inconvenience and slip it into the big stress machine, watch it grow, watch it spill and spew. Let me help you. Let me run over you in the process of trying to help where no help may be needed, when you did not ask for it, or want it. Let me wrap my helping tentacles around your problem, your indecision and denial. Let me help peel your skin right off your flesh, flay you right here to remove the small irritation you are both aware of and not.

Traumatized, I am often unconscious and will pass along some of the feeling of being traumatized to anyone who may recognize the symptoms and want to play almost dead with me. But that doesn't mean I can slow down to hear the injured and vexed voice within myself, crying for help and rescue.

Unless I am in the room. In Al-Anon no one dumps on anyone else. I've learned not to try to poison another with my history or my histrionics. I am instead called upon to be with what my current situation *appears* to be, how I feel about it, what I think it might say about me, to me. I am given time and opportunity to express my fear and sadness without damage to anyone else. I express what is real to the best of my ability. I am listened to but not commented upon.

From experience I do not expect the new ones to know all that. The new ones are allowed to bleed a little on the carpet, break down, leak out, run on and whatever they need to do to unburden the shame, fear, anger and bewilderment of their lives in the moment.

The new ones are given an information packet with names and phone numbers on it. Sometimes I add my name and number. Often, I hope they never call me. I would not know what to say, not sure I could listen without their story stirring my pot of woes, leaving me beached on *my* couch for days. I do hope they come back, again and again and again. It is only in returning to these rooms that the miracle of unfolding my life comes to be. I begin to *get it* after I have heard myself and others spill our story over and over. I also get it, that we all are living some version of the same story. I get it—after the fire is out, the floodwaters retreated, the emergency quelled, there is a long process of re-building a self, a new self, out of the ashes and debris of the old life.

I pray for us all to come alive in our pain and loss. I pray for us all to drop into the abyss of wonder, to feel what stirs, excites, diminishes, hurts or exalts us. To fly into the arms of our ailing, wailing selves, hold the pain until it rattles our bones and shatters our reserve. When tears cleanse us, these waters of redemption open the barrier of time and reconcile us to our ancestors. In this way pain is elevated from the personal to the universal. Just as personal experience flows in and from the collective consciousness, so our pain contributes, and our healing feeds the collective evolving of souls.

Progress, like growth, moves in spirals. Having to perpetually learn and practice is not equal to failure. My behaviors, anxiety and thoughts of late indicate the need to strengthen what I know and still need to practice. In the long haul of healing and recovery there is no urgency.

Since writing this piece about the fires, California has been hit by several more devastating and huge fires. The loss of life, human and animal, of property, of nature, is staggering. We are all reeling with grief.

Life inside

I am reminded I can write it all up as an experience in the woods, on the beaches, and even in the garden. Milk nature for metaphors to describe my internal environment, the one I am trying to live in, protect and provide for.

Life as a teeming zoo, a frantically growing garden, or a tree-lined street with planned landscaping. Emotions like water falling on Riyadh, or the creeping gently neglected woods, or impervious stone monuments; Zion's hot slate, Yellowstone's beige uproar from below, roaring Niagara Falls, the winding Missouri River, the veined delta, or evaporating fluids in the painted desert. Traumas heal like open, spilling calderas or slowly eroding meteorite depressions, pain perseveres as forests of Sequoia and Redwood, as soft snows falling in a quiet wood, or swaying like gentle dogwoods and elms, and on and on.

What about the more disturbing shadow properties of life? What else am I "under the influence" of? Danger in deadly amanita mushrooms, and the subtle poisons from plants that may be mistaken for harmless ones? I think I should read more about that man who died in the Alaskan wilderness because he became so weakened by starvation he could no longer discern the good from the bad plant, and realizing he had ingested the wrong green thing, said goodbye to his family, and died a cruel and painful death. What have I become so blinded to? Where are my weakened parts looking for sustenance?

And, of course, the man (is it always *men*?) who went into the wilderness to embrace the bear, and it ate him. Am I so naive about my voracious inner critic, the wilderness of self-loathing and self-managing that wants to eat me alive?

Wilderness. Right there, a great metaphor to describe the sense of vastness that might express the heft of a life trauma. Or *wildness,* as in the wild and unpredictable ride from a single word uttered in innocence, turning into a slide of razor sharpness, slashing my co-dependent, crazed self. Certainly, 'wilderness' conjures up a machete-wielding struggle, white knuckled survival. Children of alcoholics know all about all that: they have already been eaten by mean, blood-thirsty bears; drowned by flash floods of a drunk parents' runaway emotions; been left out in the wet and cold, the hot and dry, the scary trees, or the car on the dark street. We've been abandoned to the wilderness of our own family system, without any survival equipment, untethered, and certainly no direction home.

Today I worry about sustaining intimacy with my love partner as the petty tyrants inside try to get me to run away. To where or to what I do not know. I'm in a place where trauma thumps her bass drum defiantly, sending her pounding rhythms across the forest floor, up through my feet, to shake my stand and change the tone of my self-inquiry.

The trick is to notice, without prejudice, or with what my friend calls "right distance," my tendency to get smaller inside, to pull up the welcome mat and retreat into a wounded, darkened grotto of my inner environment, into the hidden understory of my small self. To consciously *roam* these interiors, as I chop wood and carry water in the outer world, to note their subtle shadings and tones, breezes and moistures, is a new freedom most welcome to my aching eyes, straining ears and otherwise wracked senses. I remember to live in the world, and to live within relationships that need me to come out, *be* out, inter-relate.

Sometimes I go away in my life, I recede and pull up my tidal skirts so they do not touch anyone or anything. I need to be in a private pool of inquiry: to feel a question arising out of ordinary events, taking me deeper down—not for easy answers, but for ideas, insights and sense material to bring to the surface. My watery edge sneaks up the beach where others are playing, talking, engaging, and listens, then recedes back down into the opaque depths to digest. Perhaps when the tide next rolls in I will gleefully crash up onto the beach to play, brimming with life.

Grace

I heard a friend say she was exchanging her magical thinking with thoughts of grace. I love grace. Grace brings the whole of heaven down to earth. I feel it in my toes; it gets in and walks with me, works with me, especially when I work with someone else. Grace allows me to put aside my fear that I may not have the clarity or presence to guide another human out of her misery.

Grace be with me today. I am hurting. Sometimes my anger, my righteous indignation, does not allow me to feel how deeply hurt I am, how the pain of life and the twist of relationship can cause such a deep wound to open in me that I prance around the edges of it, guarding it with the dance of anger. Anger is my special voodoo for many situations I cannot control. Anger allows me to focus on the other (something I am especially good at anyway), to drill holes in another soul from the safe distance of my angry, offended self. I make it about anything but that I have collapsed into an old, scary place where the sun don't shine and I do not know how long I will be there.

Grace be with me today with time. Being wounded takes up enormous amounts of time, gobbles attention that could be donated to worthy causes, helping others with worse problems than mine. Time inside my head, time inside the other's head, time avoiding grief, and when I am ready to let down the defenses of anger, time is needed to bang my head at the wailing wall of life, to make it hurt to make me cry so I will keep at it and eventually touch into the true pain of my predicament.

Life takes time. Life *is* time, wrapped around the lollypop of my self, being licked away, one layer at a time, until I am down to the stick, the papery, compressed, flavorless stick of my uncertain being.

There was a long period in my adult life when I was never alone, or not for long alone. As if I needed the other to confirm me, to show me my feet on this planet, my purpose, my prose and poetry. Then somewhere around forty-five I let it all go. I let go of being in relationship, looking for partners, trying to figure it all out through them. I stopped producing hormones to fetch another fish from the sea. I felt I had become poisonous to any and all relationships and needed only to pull back, out of the fray, get myself clean, and detox from lovers and from thinking I knew anything about love. Being in love is not all downhill release the brakes kind of nonsense. If I release my brakes, I end up on my knees down a dark road, hands skinned to the bone from having moved too fast to see the trees closing in around me.

I went back to Al-Anon meetings. I watched myself. I watched from a place deep inside, where I could be in the world, but not of the world. I watched my head turn toward something—a man, a woman, a thing, an idea—and I watched and breathed in the aroma of the thing without moving a muscle toward it. No flirtations, no gestures to be mistaken for interest in another human, unless there were no strings attached, and the human was a friend. I attended to my friendships, poured love and caring into friendships. At the same time, I craved solitude.

I healed, mostly by breaking my old habit of diving in first before testing the water. I recovered from the pain and confusion of being in relationships and marriages and carrying my baggage from man to man, to women, back to men, stuffing more in and dragging it to the next post. I left the bags somewhere, after time and grace had worn them out, their contents no longer relevant, spilled out and flung into the branches of trees, swept down creek beds and rolled down roadsides.

I cleansed through practices—meditation, shamanic healing, reading and direct work with my own energy—until I felt clean, free and clear of "all that" business. But feeling free, I wandered into a friendship with a new face, a what-else-can-we-experience-face that pulled on the strings of my self-inquiry, and so here I have entered into the messiness of relationship again, after more than twenty-five years on the outside, not looking in.

Grace be with me in this love thing.

**I understand God best not as a being,
but a divine *state* of being.**

—Angel B.

**True beauty can emerge at the most vigorous
threshold where the oppositions in life
confront and engage each other…
Beauty does not belong exclusively to the
regions of light and loveliness, cut off from
conflict and conversation of oppositions.
The vigor and vitality of beauty derives precisely
from the heart of difference.**

—John O'Donohue

Relation ship

"Sometimes obliqueness is a way to get at something directly; sometimes obliquely is the most direct way." —Me

Where was I that I came back and had this thought? It is an expression of consciousness that uses ordinary events and circumstances to turn over some deeply held rocks, to see what lies beneath. I have these experiences often, sometimes I write about them, I note them, they are a way the veil between the levels of consciousness thins allowing me to peer in and see or sense something, where connections form that were not there before. I feel my brain reconsolidating its memories and awareness, as I come up with new insights.

Often, looking directly into the fire one sees only fire and no subtlety. The fire is so central that no other understanding can make its way in. My love and I were at an impasse: we had had an unpleasant misunderstanding and I disappeared for a week, which produced fear and anger in him, while in me, well pretty much the same. He scared me bad, and I left, not knowing what else to do. I was self-protective. Even covered my front windows—did not want anyone looking in. In the same way I sometimes protect people from knowing what I know about me because I know they will never again un-know what they have learned.

I don't seem to be able to resist or deflect his stuff about me. I can't just say to myself, 'that's not about me, that's about him,' what he thinks he hears and sees. I can't remember my own mantras: *your opinion of me is none of my business* and *not about me.* I think if I know his grief about me is *his* stuff, I can attend better, won't take it on, and I won't try to make his perspective central to my life, correct myself to fit his vision.

Taking it on as my problem is called *vanity* in one of the Al-anon books. It says taking someone's stuff *on*, it is an act of ego or vanity—his world becomes all about me, I assume authority with his problem, as if I created it, as if I can solve it. I do see the relevance. His wounded child calls my wounded child out to play, and there is the root of the trouble. I am not the cause of his wounded child and he is not the cause of mine. I am sitting in a shit storm of shame and guilt—look what I did to my family? Look what I did to my*self*?

He sits in his own shit storm and it colors what he thinks he sees in me. Maybe that is *his* vanity, his ego-wounding, that thinks he should be the center of my world, I should care more about his feelings in that moment than I do about mine. Maybe we are both coming from our own ego-centric vortexes, like two tornadoes vying for space and air.

Oh, how stubbornly does love—or even that cunning semblance of love which flourishes in the imagination but strikes no depth of root into the heart—how stubbornly does it hold its faith, until the moment comes when it is doomed to vanish into thin mist!

—Nathaniel Hawthorne

So here we are at an impasse. And he is coming for breakfast. I am angry and fearful yet I do not jump to my own defense with all four feet. I decide that I will go work out first, then let him in and see if we can be in each other's company again. But for some reason, I put these little squiggly bits of metal and a crystal egg on the table's center line, knowing he will occupy one side and I the other.

We end up playing with the little squiggly metal things, arranging them and hanging them off each other, trying to make the crystal egg stand, and making up names for what we are creating, the way one describes clouds. At my kitchen table we play our way back into the sanctity of love. We approach our relationship *obliquely* as a way to get at something, and it proves to be the most direct way to open to a new understanding.

Nature has dreamed up absolutely everything you could possibly imagine; every shape, every color, every activity.

I think what fascinates me most, though,' I said, 'is what you can't see, what you can only intuit. The subtle stuff, like the patterns behind all the details.

...to me it's not that you're going beyond the natural world, you're just extending your definition of the natural world to include what isn't physically visible.

The Experience of a Lifetime by Carolyn North

I know what she means. The visible world of nature rocks me to my core, sometimes so grand in scope that I know I am apprehending the ultimate in a flower, a tree, or smudge of lichen. But the world below that, the worlds underneath what we can see must be stunningly intelligent, elegantly designed, if for no other reason than to feed the world we *can* see with our eyes. The patterns and rhythms of the underworld speak through the visible in color, form and balance, but we cannot see the rhythm, can only glimpse the pattern on the macro scale, though its origins are deep, dark, miniscule beyond belief. All the way down to the energy, the dance of elements and charges that performs the miracle of creating order out of what seems to be utter chaos.

In this relationship, I need to descend often into the depths below the pain that arranges my perspective. At least enough to allow the deeply organizing forces to be present, and to invite the unseen to work its magic again, bring us back to the essence of love and let that essence inform us, again, of who we are and what we bring to each other.

Chapter 7: Don't Take My Word for It...

It's useful to know some facts about alcoholism in order to see it as a disease, an affliction acted out by drinkers who may decry the many reasons for why they drink, but are in fact in denial, shame and grief about their addiction. Just as a person with a heart is not necessarily an expert in coronary disease, so an alcoholic is not an expert in the disease of alcoholism. Here is a random sampling of facts, figures, quotes, opinions and relevant dialog for your education.

"The surgeon general's report reaffirms what the scientific establishment has been saying for years: Addiction is a disease, not a moral failing."

From *"The Addicted Brain"* by Fran Smith,
National Geographic, 2017

"If a mere code of morals or a better philosophy of life were sufficient to overcome alcoholism, many of us would have recovered long ago…We could wish to be moral, we could wish to be philosophically comforted, in fact, we could will these things with all our might, but the needed power wasn't there. Our human resources, as marshaled by the will, were not sufficient; they failed utterly.

Lack of power, that was our dilemma. We had to find a power by which we could live, and it had to be a Power greater than ourselves. Obviously. But where and how were we to find this Power?

We found that as soon as we were able to lay aside prejudice and express even a willingness to believe in a Power greater than ourselves, we commenced to get results, even though it was impossible for any of us to fully define or comprehend that Power, which is God."

Bill W., *Alcoholics Anonymous*

"One effect of being raised in a family with an alcoholic is the deep lessons in mistrust and ill-placed control. Alcoholics who somehow managed to stop drinking but did not examine their own behaviors and beliefs, may still display attitudes and actions true to alcoholics: rigidity and righteousness, excessive control over others and situations, anxiety-driven beliefs, extreme low self-esteem and so forth..."

Susan Cheever, *Drinking in America:*
our secret history

The Drunk and Disorderly Language is deeply embedded in our culture—

Bring many names:

Binging
Blind drunk
Blitzed
Blotto
Bombed
Buzzed, got a buzz on

Crapulent: pertaining to drinking alcohol or to drunkenness

Dead drunk
Deep in one's cups
Destroyed
Drowned, as in drowned in his fishbowl
Drunk; drunk on his ass
Drunk as a skunk, as a lord
DT'd (a frightening reference to Delirium Tremens, one of the sure signs one is dying of alcoholic poisoning)

Fell off; fell off the wagon
Fucked, fucked up, fucking the fire

Gone
Good, as in "I'm good."
Guzzling

Hammered
High

Juiced

Inebriated
In his cups
In the bag, half in the bag; i.e., "When I got to the party, Rob
was half in the bag."
In the bottle
Intoxicated

Lit
Loaded; loaded to the gills
Looped
Lost, Lost Weekend-like

Messed Up
No helmet, as in "the retard's out of his helmet"

Off the wagon
On a bender: maybe a reference to "bending elbows" at
the bar
On a tear
Out of his mind, his gourd, his tree…
Over-served

Pickled
Pie-eyed
Pissed
Plastered

Plowed

Riding the night train

Sauced
Sautéed
Schnockered
Shit-canned
Shit-faced
Slammed
Sloshed
Smashed
Snot-flying drunk
Sodded
Sotted
Soused: souse, pickled German something or other
Stiff
Stiff as a priest
Stone drunk
Stoned—some are so drunk they don't know that this
expression refers to drugs
Stupid drunk
Swizzled

Tanked
Tie one on
Tight
Three sheets to the wind
Toasted, toasty
Tying one on

Under the influence
Unstable

Wacked out
Wasted
Wiped out
Wrecked

Then I woke up—

(in an) Alcoholic fugue
Alcoholic fug
Bloated drunk
Crashing, crashed
Hung over
Irish flu
Guttered
Coming down
Lost
Singing to the porcelain god
Worshipping the porcelain goddess

He or She is a _________ (frequently preceded by "fucking")

Waste-oid, as in "Joe is a fucking waste-oid."
Lush
Bar fly
Alchy
Count Drunkula
Drunkard
Idiot

Asshole
Booze Hound (dogs learn *not* to drink from one whisky bender)
Sod or Sot

Drinking Games

Beer guzzling (a popular sport on campus, resulting occasionally in death)
Pre-loading: drinking before going out to drink

Alcohol is

Booze
Hooch
Fire Water
Camel piss
Sterno
Sneaky Pete
Social Lubricant
Natty Lite (Natural Light)
Jungle Juice

Sober-as a judge?

abstemious
tee-total
dry-drunk

We toast:

Here's looking up your old address

Here's mud in your eye
Skoal
To your health
L'chaim
Chin-chin

Quotable Quotes:

"I have an allergy to alcohol. Whenever I drink, I come down with a drunk."

"I used up all my sick pay (drinking) so I called in dead."

Comedian Robin Williams compared a functioning alcoholic to a paraplegic lap-dancer

Williams proposed warning label for bottles of alcohol: "Prepare to lose yourself"

I grab from online pages and "dictionaries" and sometimes do not record the source. My apologies to whomever originally compiled these notes.

Three Sheets to the Wind

The phrase dates to 1821. The *sheet* is a reference to a rope of a sail on any sized sailing craft. To have a sheet loose in the wind is bad seamanship, to have three loose means you are not capable of controlling the boat. Occasionally you will see *one sheet to the wind* meaning half-drunk.

Mother, being a Navy gal herself, loved this term. The more she drank, the more compelled she felt to define it after saying it.

Teetotal

The *tee* stands for the letter *T*, not *tea*, and is repeated for emphasis. A *teetotaler* is emphatic about not drinking.

The word was first used (in the sense of abstaining from alcohol) at an 1833 temperance rally in England by a workingman named Richard Turner.

There is evidence that that the adverb *tee-totally* was in use in Ireland and the US before this (probably of Irish origin), but in a general sense and not specifically related to temperance. *I doubt our family ever produced a teetotaler.*

Hooch:

The name is Native American, from the Tlingit, after the Hoochinoo Indians of Alaska and distilled liquor manufactured by them.

From *Seal and Salmon Fisheries and General Resources of Alaska,* 1869:

The natives manufacture by distillation from molasses a vile, poisonous life- and soul-destroying decoction called "hoochenoo."

The clipped form appears in 1897 in M.H.E. Hayne's *Pioneers of the Klondyke:*

The manufacture of "hooch," which is undertaken by the saloon-keepers themselves, is weirdly horrible.

Reminds me of the crude rum-like drink made from coconuts, called arak, drunk by drunks in Sri Lanka, and likely anywhere coconuts are plentiful. Worst hangover of my life was from arak.

Did you know...

Prolonged, excessive use of alcohol causes insanity

The old adage that doing the same thing in the same way repeatedly is insane comes from the understanding that alcoholics and addicts repeatedly go back to their substance of choice though they know where use will take them, and it always leads to the same result.

Behind the use and the substance, the alcoholic repeats other behaviors and thoughts too, they become a machine that lives to drink, all spontaneity is suppressed and behaviors and thoughts become entrained to the need for alcohol in the body, the brain, the life. One day we may identify the organisms within the body, fed by alcohol, that we are drinking for, in the same way that we know we eat for our cells' mitochondria.

Behind the psychology of behavior is the reality of brain damage from alcoholic poisoning, insanity caused by alcohol consumption.

* * *

There is a condition called "belly beer" or Autobrewery Syndrome, when a regular drinker has created an *environment* within the gut, and experiences spontaneous drunkenness without necessarily imbibing anything.

* * *

Addiction causes hundreds of changes in brain anatomy, chemistry, and cell-to-cell signaling, including in the gaps between neurons called synapses, which are the molecular machinery for learning. By taking advantage of the brain's marvelous plasticity, addiction re-molds neural circuits to assign supreme value to cocaine or heroin or gin, at the expense of other interests such as health, work, family, or life itself. In a sense, addiction is a pathological form of learning, says Antonello Bonci, a neurologist at the National Institute on Drug Abuse. **From "The Addicted Brain" by Fran Smith, National Geographic, September 2017**

* * *

More than 200,000 people worldwide die every year from drug over-doses and drug-related illnesses, such as HIV, according to the United Nations Office on Drugs and Crime, and far more die from smoking and drinking. **Nearly one of every 20 adults worldwide is addicted to alcohol.** No one has yet counted people hooked on gambling and other compulsive activities gaining recognition as addictions.

"The Addicted Brain" by Fran Smith, National Geographic, September 2017

Alcoholics and Mental Illness

- 80% of alcoholics have underlying MD bipolar disorder and/ or depression.

"In 2014, the Centers for Disease Control issued a scath-ing summation of the damage drinking does in the United

States. The CDC reported that 88,000 adults a year die of alcohol consumption. There are also, the CDC report says, more than a million alcohol-related emergency room visits as well as 10,000 traffic fatalities a year caused by drinking."

***Drinking in America: our secret history* by Susan Cheever**

Citation for the 5 top ways "more than 90% of 12-14 year old kids obtain alcohol for free":

14%: from an unrelated adult, such as a neighbor

15%: from an adult relative, including an older sibling

15%: from a parent or guardian

16%: at their own home, often from an unlocked liquor cabinet

19% from another underage person, like a friend

National Survey on Drug Use and Health

Conventional wisdom about Children of Alcoholics, or COAs

- Become adults too early: They take over for Mom (and/or Dad); guard or protect the younger siblings; become best friends with parents instead of remaining children (it's a benefit to the alcoholic to have an ally in the family, an ally in denial).

- Lose their own childhoods, often leading to "driven-ness" in professions, problems with intimacy and relationships; they often experience a sense of "lost self" in relationships.

- Become professional helpers: about 30% of all professional helpers (and healers) are from alcoholic families.

- Develop a skewed sense of normal.

- Daughters of alcoholics usually have intimacy issues, especially with men; they tend to leave home early. Conflicts from family life tend to manifest into habits of worrying.

- COA's suffer from perpetual uncertainty from living with an alcoholic, who like a volcano, can erupt and destroy at any time.

- Most children of alcoholics fear passing on alcoholism, Manic-Depressive syndrome or depression to their kids.

- 85-95% of COAs do *not* manifest severe mental illnesses (in my own case, I *decided* to be one of the 95% vs becoming one of the 5%)

There's an old saying that letting someone rob you of self-esteem is like letting the waiter eat your supper.

Problem drinking affects 33 Million

By Lindsay Tanner

Associated press, June 14, 2015 *Press Democrat*, Santa Rosa, California

"Alcohol problems affect almost 33 million adults and most have never sought treatment," according to a government survey that suggests rates have increased in recent years.

The study is the first national estimate based on a new term, "alcohol use disorder," in a widely used psychiatric handbook that was updated in 2013.

Five things to know about the research...in the journal JAMA psychiatry:

Defining problems

The revised handbook, the DSM-5, defined problem drinkers or those with the disorder as people with at least two of the 11 symptoms, including drinking that harms performance at work, school or home, frequent hangovers and failed attempts to limit drinking. Mild problems involved 2 to 3 symptoms; severe involved at least six symptoms. The new handbook combined alcohol abuse and dependence, which had been separate disorders, added craving as one symptom and eliminated alcohol—related legal problems as another.

The numbers

Researchers from the National Institute on Alcohol Abuse and

Alcoholism asked 36,000 adults during 2012 or 2013 about lifetime drinking habits including current or within the past year. About 14% of adults were current or recent problem drinkers, or nearly 33 million nationally, and 30% – almost 69 million – had been at some point in their lives. Mild drinking problems were the most common, while 14% had never experienced severe drinking problems.

Heavy drinking

Nearly 40% of adults surveyed said they had engaged in binge drinking – downing at least five drinks in a day at least once in the past year, up from 31% in the earlier survey. Even heavier drinking also increased but was less common.

Who's drinking?

Drinking problems were most prevalent among men, whites and Native Americans. Low-income adults, those younger than 30 and those who never married also had relatively high rates. The West and Midwest had higher rates of problem drinking than other regions.

Stigma and denial

Dr. George Koob, director of the federal agency that did the survey, said "it is unclear why problem drinking has increased, but many people underestimate the dangers of excessive alcohol. Many won't seek help because of "stigma and denial," and many don't realize that medications and behavior treatments can help."

* * *

Alcohol-impaired driving remains the deadliest and costliest danger on U.S. roads today, the report states. Every day in the United States, 29 people die in an alcohol-impaired driving crash — one death every 49 minutes — making it a persistent public health and safety problem.

National Academy of Sciences, Engineering and Medicine, Washington, DC Lifted from MADD website

From Janet G. Woititz, Ed.D,

Adult Children of Alcoholics often:

- Guess at what normal behavior is
- Have difficulty following a project through from beginning to end
- Lie when it would be just as easy to tell the truth
- Judge themselves without mercy
- Have difficulty having fun
- Take themselves very seriously
- Have difficulty with intimate relationships
- Overreact to changes over which they have no control
- Constantly seek approval and affirmation
- Feel that they're different from other people
- Are super responsible or super irresponsible
- Are extremely loyal, even in the face of evidence that the loyalty is undeserved
- Are impulsive—They tend to lock themselves into a course of action without giving serious consideration to alternative

behaviors or possible consequences. This impulsively leads to confusion, self-loathing, and loss of control over their environment. In addition, they spend an excessive amount of energy cleaning up the mess.

Drunks and Users (Experts)

Notable alcoholic writers include James Thurber and EB White, John Cheever, Raymond Carver, Robert Frost, Wallace Stevens, Edna St. Vincent Malay, Raymond Chandler, Baudelaire, David Foster Wallace, Edgar Allan Poe (a notable exception among the 19th century pantheon of tee-totaling writers) Sinclair Lewis, Brendan Behan, Djuna Barnes, Dawn Hall, Dorothy Parker…

Actor Jack Lemmon to James Lipton before a live audience of the Actors Studio: "I am an alcoholic," he repeated over and over and over again until Lipton understood Lemmon was not talking about or acting out his role in "Days of Wine and Roses," but owning the reality of his life.

Elton John abused alcohol and drugs for 16 years.

Amy Winehouse died of alcoholic poisoning in 2011, age 27.

"This one's a warning not to think of a junkie as a complete functioning human being. Heroin should've killed me about five times, but it never did. My kids suffered from their father being an addict. I think there's no way they can't. People take drugs to be in control. They want to short-circuit any risk that they might take in life, any uncertainty, any anxiety. They just want to find the chemical route, to just push the button that gets the final result. So all of your relationships suffer, no question about it."

Singer-songwriter, and heroin addict, James Taylor, "Rolling Stone magazine", 2015.

– 194 –

Alcoholics can be extra nice when sober

Bad things happen with Alcoholics…

My brother's best friend, H. was living on the streets, he had become a zombie for booze, and automaton for alcohol. He went into a blood donation clinic to make some money so he could buy some booze. By then, he had donated blood hundreds of times so he could continue drinking. On this day the intake person looked up and asked, "How old a man are you?" And H. had to think first about himself and his age, but then it dawned on him that she had called him a *man*, and for a moment he realizes he has no attachment to being a man, he has lost the sense that he *is* a man, but he knows somewhere inside that he is. This tiny recognition begins the process of coming out of years of denial and horrible binge drinking, and back into sobriety. H. has lived sober for over 30 years, and his life is now helping others with meditation and in getting and staying sober.

A woman I know had been ritually, sexually and physically abused as a child.

She had three brothers, one alcoholic parent and another mostly absent parent. The youngest brother, about 6 when the abuse began, learned to participate in the melee, though he was quite a bit younger than his older siblings, and younger than my friend. He learned well from his older brothers, how to corner and capture his sister, how to taunt her, threaten her, and eventually physically overcome her defenses. She was tormented, humiliated through nudity and exposure, sexually abused in every egregious way one can imagine, then often beaten for being a girl, being scared, being angry… She was threatened into silence. Alcohol, even with the youngest child, not only made this horrible ongoing torture possible, it provided just the excuse the older brothers needed to accept their own behavior toward their sister, and the warping, damaging effect on their younger brother, who, at 20, committed suicide.

According to another friend of mine, alcohol played a key role in her experience of rape and ongoing abusive manipulation at the hands of her church priest. The priest molested boys and girls in his parish for years, and when confronted, blamed his alcohol use.

DEAR ABBY   By Jeanne Phillips

"Addiction is Real"

Dear Abby: I had my last cigarette and drink of alcohol 50 years ago. Back then, excessive drinking, smoking, over eating, etc., were signs of weak will, sin, bad upbringing and who knows what else. Fortunately, the pendulum swung making it possible for millions of people to get into recovery for what we now know is a *disease* – addiction. Unfortunately the pendulum is now swinging back again.

Now everyone has a "disease" they cannot control, giving them an excuse to drink too much, over eat—the list goes on. Sadly, this business of taking no responsibility for one's own health and – worse yet – often blaming someone or something else for the problem takes away from those who are taking responsibility for themselves. Getting by with a third DUI or being excused for being late to work for the fourth time because of one's "disease" all contribute to the stigma many of us have been fighting for so long.

Addiction is a *disease*, and there are many avenues of recovery: mental, spiritual, medical, philosophical. What they have in common is they require a commitment to getting well.

Abby, I want to reinforce your dedication to promoting personal responsibility. It is desperately needed!

Roberta Meyer, former president, National Council on Alcohol and Drug Dependence

Dear Roberta: your letter contains many important truths. As I've said before, the first step in solving a problem is admitting there is one and deciding to do something about it. The same is true for addiction. That's why Twelve Step programs are so effective—people gain emotional support from others who are traveling the same path to recovery.

An American History lesson

"By the mid 1920s, the American government was at its wit's end. The era's strict Prohibition laws had proved futile. Americans were still drinking; they were just doing so on the sly, frequenting speakeasies and buying alcohol from crime syndicates. Gangs would steal large quantities of industrial alcohol—used for everything from fueling machines to sterilizing instruments—then readistill the hooch to remove impurities before putting it on the market. In its effort to fight back the bureau of prohibition came up with a shocking idea: what if it poisoned the industrial alcohol supply?

In 1926, the federal government bought into the idea, issuing regulations that required manufacturers to make industrial alcohol more lethal. The new formulas included mercury salts, benzene and kerosene, and the results were chilling. Alcohol related deaths skyrocketed, with officials attributing more than 1000 deaths to the program in its first year alone. People were outraged.

"The United States government must be charged with the moral responsibility for the deaths," said New York City medical examiner Charles Norris, one of the measure's most outspoken foes.

The government held firm on its position even as the body count rose. In New York City, 400 people died the first year. 700 died the next, and the pattern was replicated in cities across the country. Yet prohibitionists continued to defend the law. The anti-saloon league, Norris's frequent sparring partner, fired back: "Dr. Norris should logically next demand palatable varnish and potable shellac." Nebraska's Omaha Bee asked, "Must Uncle Sam guarantee safety for souses?"

It took more than 10,000 American deaths and a furious public backlash for the government to quietly end its "chemists war." But it wasn't until sometime around 1933, when the regulations were phased out quietly, that what Norris had dubbed "our national experiment in extermination" was officially over."

July/August 2013 mentalfloss.com

Numerous situations are described In **Susan Cheever's Drinking in America: our secret history,** *where the country itself was in great danger under an alcoholic president:*

In one scenario "where nuclear powers were squaring off, military staging in the Middle East as a Soviet-backed Arab army clashed with American backed Israeli army and the threat of nuclear war became a reality." Kissinger tried to call the president, and was told by Alexander Haig he wasn't available. …Kissinger called a meeting in the White House Situation room, military was put on alert at US airbases. Writes Anthony Sommers, "B-52s were loaded with nuclear weapons and lined up nose to tail. In missile silos launch commanders buckled themselves into their chairs. Nuclear arms submarines sped to secret positions off the Soviet coast." The president was asleep, or apparently drunk, or passed out, or had taken a sleeping pill because even one drink could make him appear and feel drunk."

Consider the numbers

Lots of people die using drugs and alcohol. What the books and the reports and the studies cannot really say is how many of us actually drink to excess. How could we possibly know that? By liquor sales? Combined with bar sales? The unlikely scenario of people reporting on themselves? It's got to be a huge number of people out there every night consuming too much booze, no matter how you wish to tally the numbers.

Since denial is a major feature of alcoholic behavior, and alcohol use is under-reported or goes altogether unmentioned to the family physician, there are no true numbers to tell us how many alcoholics there might be in the U.S. And, no sources I could find to help us speculate on the numbers of people *affected* by alcoholism. However, the National Institutes of Health, Alcohol Abuse and Alcoholism, estimates that 14.1 million adult alcoholics are alive in America at any given time.

Bruce Gibbs, PhD, reasons that an average of five people are close enough to be deeply affected by the alcoholic. Using the NIH estimate for numbers of alcoholics, that's 70 million people related to and affected by the alcoholic. That seems like a reasonable, if still an *un*reasonable, number of affected people.

We might further speculate that one quarter to one third of the 70 million are children of alcoholics—young and older. Maybe one half or more of the 70 million, some 35 million, are family. Imagine a city like New York with 4.3 times as many people as currently reside there, all wandering in that desert confused, angry, hurting and clueless and in need of help and direction.

Just for the 88,000 who *died* from alcoholic poisoning in 2014, that's 440,000 (just a little over the population of Oakland, California or Portland city, Oregon). Nearly half a million loved ones left to wonder why. These are people who were close enough to the alcoholic to have been deeply emotionally affected by their drinking, years and years of drinking, of showing up drunk to or entirely missing every important family function, of coming home in a drunken stupor, of returning to the emergency room again and again with problems related to drinking, of ending up in alleyways and on street corners, in parks or wandering the streets aimlessly, of the missed days at work, the missed school and sporting events in their kids' lives, the drunken rages and violence, the missed opportunities for love, intimacy and support. And some got a phone call from the police in the middle of the night, to come to the morgue to identify their teenaged son or daughter, who had died from binge drinking at a party.

And that's not counting the 10,000 who died in alcohol-related accidents, in a car wrapped around a tree or destroyed on the freeway, and who may or not have been drinking, but were killed by someone who drank too much that day. Or the probable millions who simply drink too much. Let us also consider numbers of people in Al-Anon, numbers of people in therapy to understand and deal with the drunk, and numbers of people *not* in therapy, suffering and wandering in their lives, wondering what they could do differently to change the situation, influence their sister, brother, mother, father, spouse, friend to let up on the drinking already. That's a lot of us no matter what way you think of it.

Most kids get alcohol free—many from their own homes. We don't keep the stuff under lock and key. And our kids watch the drinking, and the drinker. They can see there is a special relationship going on between the drinker and his substance (or the drug user and his substance). It is this *relating to the substance* that they see over and over again, a the drama and results, the changes occurring in the drinker or user, the special, unavailable places their parents go when they use. This is why M. Scott Peck, PhD, says that children learn about relationship from *observing their parents* relating to their substance.

And if you need more numbers, Mothers Against Drunk Drivers' got 'em. Visit MADD.org for the full research on each of these statements.

MADD's street creds:

- In the United States, the number of drunk driving deaths has been cut in half since MADD was founded in 1980.

MADD tracks drinking, drugging and driving in this country:

- About one-third of all drivers arrested or convicted of drunk driving are repeat offenders.
- Only time will sober a person up. Drinking strong coffee, exercising or taking a cold shower will not help.

It's clear we need to take it to young teens: they don't know not to start drinking before their brains mature, and before the "age of reason" has dawned within them:

- Kids who start drinking young are seven times more likely to be in an alcohol-related crash.
- About a quarter of car crashes with teens involve an underage drinking driver. Ninety-five percent of the 14 million people who are alcohol dependent began drinking before the legal age of 21.
- Over 40% of all 10th graders drink alcohol.
- Over a quarter of 8th graders have tried alcohol.
- Youth who start drinking before age 15 years are **six times** more likely to develop alcohol dependence or abuse later in life than those who begin drinking at or after age 21 years.

MADD's grimmer statistics:

- 4300 people are killed each year due to teen alcohol use—more than all other drugs combined.
- Youth who start drinking before age 15 are 6 times more likely to develop alcohol dependence or abuse later in life.
- Car crashes are the **Number 1** leading cause of death in teenagers.
- 1 in 4 car crashes with teenagers involve an underage drunk driver.

Case in point:

From *The Press Democrat*, Santa Rosa, California, February 2018

Headline: "Teen gets 6 years in drunken crash that killed her sister"
By Joseph Serna
Los Angeles Times

Subheading: Stockton resident livestreamed losing control of vehicle

A California teen who was driving drunk as she livestreamed a crash on social media that killed her younger sister was sentenced to more than six years and four months in prison on Thursday, officials said.

Obdulia Sanchez, 19, pleaded guilty last month to gross vehicular manslaughter, driving under the influence and child endangerment in connection with the July 2017 crash that killed her sister and gained global attention.

The Stockton resident recorded video of herself on Instagram, **live** behind the wheel of a 2003 Buick as her 14-year-old sister, Jacqueline Sanchez, and a second 14-year-old girl sat in the back seat.

The alarming video showed Sanchez losing control of her vehicle and crashing.

Moments later, she showed the body of her sister and said: "I killed my sister, OK. I know I am going to jail for life, all right? This is the last thing that I wanted to happen, OK?"

The CHP said Sanchez was driving north of Los Banos when she swerved off the road and over corrected. The car then veered across the road, crashed into a wire fence and rolled into a field.

The two girls, who were not wearing seatbelts, were ejected from the vehicle, CHP said."

Random sampling from the *Press Democrat,*
November, 2017

Headline: Grimm start to season of DUI enforcement: 4 people have died since November 5 in suspected drunken driving crashes

"The series of fatal collisions peak November 5, with a Sunday night crash on Lakeville Highway that killed Paulette Quinta an Oakley resident and 21-year-old Sonoma State University student. Driver, Logo Tevaseu, 35, of Santa Rosa, who authorities said crossed over double yellow lines and slammed head-on into Quiba's vehicle, had a 2012 DUI conviction and was driving with more than double the legal blood alcohol limit according to the CHP. They arrested him on suspicion of murder.

On November 14 at about 7:45 AM in Boyes Hot Springs resident Estafania Soto, 27, was driving her daughter, Kaliyah Adkins, 7 years old, to school in Sonoma when they were struck by a vehicle on Highway 12. The mother died in the crash and the girl died days later. The CHP arrested driver Jose Manuel Lopez-Perez, 25, of Santa Rosa on two counts of murder. He had a DUI conviction in 2013, and was also alleged to have crossed double yellow lines to make an illegal pass.

Late Sunday morning, Lakeport resident Teodulo Tovar, Jr., 29, was headed South on Highway 101 in Petaluma when he failed to see warning signs he had traveled into a construction zone. He crashed into a concrete abutment head on. The impact killed his father, Teodulo Tovar, 66, and badly injured his 57-year old mother, both of Lakeport. The driver remained hospitalized Tuesday with life threat-ening injuries and has been arrested on suspicion of manslaughter and felony drunken driving. The CHP said he told officers he been drinking and smoking marijuana that morning.

As well as a cluster of fatal crashes, local CHP officers…have reported spikes in DUI arrests. In the first three weeks of November, CHP officers arrested 62 suspected DUI drivers on Sonoma county highways and unincorporated roads. That's up from 56 arrests in 2015 and 44 in 2016."

Included in that tally of DUI arrests in Sonoma county is the story of a Petaluma woman in the Sonoma county jail suspected of drunk driving after running a red light and hitting another vehicle, according to Petaluma police.

"Danielle Carter, 32, was arrested by Petaluma police Sunday night, suspected of felony DUI causing an injury and driving with a suspended license stemming from an earlier DUI arrest. An investigation determined Carter failed to stop for a traffic light and caused the crash. Her bail was set at $100,000."

The above articles appeared in the same edition of the Press Democrat (Sonoma County, California). Each is a random sampling of the tally of DUI arrests and the injuries and fatalities caused. A few days later, I read about a man who killed 4 people and injured 7, fled the scene (makes you wonder how drunk he was if he had the wherewithal to flee), and was arrested an hour later, charged with vehicular manslaughter x 4. Pick up any newspaper, anywhere in the US, and you will find similar stories, similar losses, spikes in DUI arrests, accidents and the death and injury they cause. What is often omitted from these stories is the trail of destruction and awful grief overwhelming the families and communities left behind.

Descansos

In almost every community across America you will see "descansos" or crash sites adorned with flowers, photos, stuffed animals and trinkets or crude white crosses, marking the site where someone died. Right on that spot, someone died in a crash. In most of these crashes, as they say in the papers, alcohol was involved.

To get another hit of humor/horror—

The Darwin Awards

From the Darwin Awards website…

"It's that time again… The Darwin Awards are finally out, the annual honor given to the persons who did the gene pool the biggest service by killing themselves in the most extraordinarily stupid way."

Here's a winning example—

A young Canadian man, searching for a way of getting drunk cheaply, because he had no money with which to buy alcohol, mixed gasoline with milk. Not surprisingly, this concoction made him ill, and he vomited into the fireplace in his house. The resulting explosion and fire burned his house down, killing both him and his sister.

Darwin Award: Roadkill

A group of friends was stranded beside the freeway when their automobile ran out of gas. The weather was terrible, and despite their frantic efforts, nobody would stop to help them. Eventually one member of the group became so frustrated that he stomped to the middle of the freeway and sprawled out across the road.

His friends tried to get him to move, but he yelled back, "I could sleep here!" Indeed he could. He was permanently lulled to sleep by an Audi sports car that hit and dragged him sixty yards to his death.

The police found several empty beer bottles lying around the car. We can only hope the twenty-one-year-old was drunk enough to dull the pain of the impact.

Darwin Award: The Smoking Gun

Two drunks were goofing around, when one challenged the other to shoot him with cigarette butts "to see what it would feel like." His friend obligingly loaded an antique rifle with cigarette butts, placing black powder behind the butts to make sure they left the barrel of the gun. He then shot his friend from a distance of seven feet. The projectiles penetrated the ribcage of the thirty-one-year-old who had issued the challenge, and he died of three cigarette butts to the heart.

The gene pool is in trouble!

Darwin commentaries: "Cigarettes are bad for your health." "It's true—Smoking Kills." "More ammunition for the antismoking campaign."

From The Press Democrat, Friday, August 24, 2018

Headline: Safest level of alcohol to drink? None

"Worldwide study says no amount of drinking is good for your health."

"…a massive study co-authored by 512 researchers from 243 institutions, a database of more than a thousand alcohol studies and data sources, as well as death and disability records from 195 countries and territories between 1990 and 2016, (and) published in the prestigious journal the Lancet," concluded "to minimize health risks, the optimal amount of alcohol someone should consume is none." (from 2 paragraphs)

"The report found that 2.8 million people across the globe died in 2016 of alcohol-related causes…"

"For people aged 15 to 49, alcohol is the leading risk factor for experiencing a negative health outcome." *Such as death.*

From the Centers for Disease Control, www.cdc.gov

The *Guidelines* also note that some people should not drink alcohol at all, including:

- Women who are or may be pregnant.
- People younger than age 21.
- People who have certain medical conditions or are taking certain medications that can interact with alcohol.
- Recovering alcoholics or people unable to control the amount they drink.

- People who are doing things that require skill, coordination, and alertness, such as driving a car.
- The *Guidelines* also state that women who are breastfeeding should talk with their health care provider about alcohol consumption.

Excessive alcohol use is responsible for approximately 88,000 deaths in the United States each year and $249 billion in economic costs in 2010. Excessive alcohol use includes:

- Binge drinking (defined as consuming 4 or more alcoholic beverages per occasion for women or 5 or more drinks per occasion for men).
- Heavy drinking (defined as consuming 8 or more alcoholic beverages per week for women or 15 or more alcoholic beverages per week for men).
- Any drinking by pregnant women or those younger than age 21.

Last word

It seems only fair to include a poignant story about my mother's inherent kindness to balance the other stories about her dysfunctional self; knowing and remembering this "other side" moves me still in deep gratitude and awe.

I came home after graduation from high school in 1968. Mother was working most nights at Dulles Airport in the Air Mail Facility and had many good friends there. One was a hippie she wanted me to meet. J was very fond of my mother and they enjoyed many interesting conversations about a variety of things. They may have gone out drinking together (no idea). J and I hit it off well enough and we had a few dates. Usually he drank and I did not. We smoked pot, another substance I could not handle too well, and watched movies. He was a bit older than me, maybe 6-8 years older. I don't feel I ever got to know this man at all, we just hung out with each other, me being awkward, him being aloof and fond of making poetic references I did not understand.

One evening at home, while watching TV, J made his move on me. I squirmed and refused but not very loudly because Mother was sleeping in the next room. These days we would call what he did a "date rape." Immediately after I wanted nothing more to do with him and at the same time felt at fault for what happened.

I got pregnant. Mother was sad about it but understanding, we cried together. She was also angry with herself for leaving me alone with J. She wanted to be overtly angry with him, call him out at work, but I asked her not to tell him I had gotten pregnant because I did not want him to have any claim on me or the baby. I was tempted to seek an abortion but just could not bring myself to think of that possibility.

As the pregnancy progressed I went to a Florence Crittenden Home for unwed mothers in Washington, DC to finish my term. While there I arranged for the baby to be adopted by a Jewish family in the area and felt certain I had made a wise choice. In fact, choosing adoption and to use Jewish Social Services to find the parents were the only choices in this entire predicament I *knew* to be right.

After my son was born we both came back to the Crittenden Home for convalescence. My sister warned me not to hold my baby, and for-god-sake not to nurse him, or I would never be able to give him up after bonding with him. She scared me so badly I refused to even see him in the nursery. At the same time I felt deeply conflicted from choosing not to interact with him. Three or four days later, his new parents came to pick him up and I went home.

Several years later my mother and I talked about the child we both had come to call "Moses" and the circumstances surrounding his first days on Earth. After his birth, she had been disturbed to hear I would not see him, but she also understood my fear. Every day my son was in the nursery, Mother came to visit. I thought she just came to see me, but without ever mentioning it, she also went into the nursery, both on the way in to see me, and again on the way out. She picked up her grandson, held him lovingly, gently. Sometimes there was a bottle to feed him. Mostly she just spent time with him. Sung to him. Told him we called him Moses. Told him how beautiful he was, told him we loved him and would never forget him. She also told him who his people were: I imagine she used the words "pioneer stock" or even "Southern aristocracy" to describe us, his true family, as she often did when talking about our people to me. Perhaps she mentioned she was an artist and his grandpa an architect-builder, as I might have. She cried over him and allowed her heart to break along with mine. I was so relieved to hear about this awesome act of charity and love, I felt a huge burden of guilt lifted from me.

Thirty-five years after he was born, it came time for my son to search for his birth family. He was not at all interested in finding his father, only in finding me and other possible siblings. I relished the opportunity to tell Rob all about his grandmother, and how she had the courage and compassion to do what I could not. She had simply wanted him to know he was loved.

I knew since childhood my mother had the capacity for compassion. Her drinking and life woes weighed so heavily on our family that I mostly forgot her ability to show such kindness. From the moment she first recounted her experience with my son, I knew there was something I could do for her: believe in her ability to get sober. Someday, somehow, she could do it. And though life with her would remain challenging for many more years, I had tucked away this other knowledge of her as a human being, and would never give up on her because of it. She had six sober years before she died.

As I said in an earlier chapter: My mother was one of the kindest people I have ever known, and she abandoned us all for her alcoholic stupors. She was one of the most interesting, intelligent and well-read women I have ever met, and she offered little guidance or support for our own development. She could be rational, cautious and caring, and she put us at risk many times because she was drinking. She was loving, but not of herself; giving but not *to* herself; seemingly humble, but proud of her ability to have handled people who enabled her addiction and denial...

Just like the rest of us, she was a multi-dimensional being. Just as all sorts of people have heart disease or kidney failure, all sorts of people have alcoholism. Look at the alcoholics in your life. Can you imagine one day they might get sober, live softer inside and be more available to you? (as opposed to hope they will stop drinking). Many alcoholics cannot imagine a way out, a way to live without alcohol, so maybe it's up to us, children and grandchildren and friends of alcoholics, to imagine *for* them, a possible sober life.

If you or a loved one are struggling with substance use or addiction, contact the *Substance Abuse and Mental Health Services Administration (SAMHSA) National Helpline* at **1-800-662-4357** for information on support and treatment facilities in your area.

Epilogue

I had not planned to include an epilogue in this memoir. In fact, I was finished writing and in final editing, planning a cover with my photographer husband. But my sister, Dotsie, whom I call "Dee" in this memoir, died. She was 77. She died of liver failure due to alcoholism: the latest tragedy in our family, due to alcohol. Her daughter, Emily, died 10 years before, in 2013, by having a head-on collision, which also killed a young man, while she was intoxicated and likely passed out at the wheel. She was 49. Her story is the Prologue. So, you might say, my niece and my sister get the first and the last words in this memoir about family alcoholism.

Here's the lineup of known alcoholics: at least one great grandfather, both grandfathers and one grandmother, both my parents, 8 aunts and uncles, at least 2 cousins, my sister and her daughter. My mother died at 72 from heart failure due to emphysema, but her health was destroyed first by alcohol. Her surgeon said if he had known her liver had shrunken to the size and texture of a walnut, he never would have operated to save her life by repairing a strangled intestine. If the rest of this memoir did not illustrate it clearly enough, it bears repeating: Alcoholism is a family disease.

My sister, Dotsie, was brilliant. A Ph.D. scientist and professor, who became a gate-keeper to medical school. If you didn't pass her anatomy classes, you didn't go to medical school! She was hard core in many ways. She imparted her precision, preferences, and perfection-istic tendencies upon her two children, ran her home like a military hospital, and held the highest standards for everyone around her. I often felt like an outcast slob, like my mother. Everyone should live like Dotsie, with her just-so home and her ultra-high standards.

To me, she was a perfect example of the Queen archetype. She could be imperious, and impervious to the needs of others. She was a natural leader of others from about 5 years old, and could get all the kids in the neighborhood gathered into her schemes. But she also tri-angulated relationships with our friends, pulling them away from me if she wanted play with them, or stranding those same friends, leaving them to me (and Brent) as second-best playmates. She told us what to do, in kind and clever terms if we were among our friends, or in "no uncertain terms" if it was just me. She had been our "other mother" since about 7, and acted as a guardian, watchdog, and trendsetter for me and all the kids on our block.

Even as a young child, my sister was a clever schemer. When we went to school in September, the weather was just right for the beach. It was hard to go to school when we were still in summer mode. Dotsie devised a plan. First, we packed our bathing suits into our lunch pails and covered them with a napkin, before placing our pea-nut butter sandwiches and orange on top. Then, we made for Candy's house next door. Every weekday morning, our friend, Candy, was charged with the task of opening the huge doors on the garage in front of her house. A little while later Candy's mother, Jean, would come down the walkway, pull the car out of the garage, rush to close the doors, and speed away to work. So, under Dotsie's direction, all us kids gathered one day at Candy's and watched as she opened the garage doors. As a group, we then walked first toward the school, but turned right instead of left at the corner and then again at the next corner, and the next, to come back around to the garage from down the street, where we would not be seen by Jean. We entered the garage and climbed the ladder up to the loft at the back. We hid behind the boxes stored up there until we heard the front door slam. We could hear Jean's heels tap, tap, tap down the sidewalk as she approached the garage. We were hushed by Dotsie, who glared at me, making me be absolutely still and not breathe. Hard to do in that hot, stuffy loft, just under the redwood rafters.

After Jean closed the doors and drove away, we escaped the stifling garage and ran down to the beach. We hung out all day, played in the surf, ate our sandwiches, and played some more. Dotsie knew when it was time to come home. She always knew. We trudged back up the hill toward our street, but again went around several streets until we came to the top of ours, then turned down toward home with the other kids from school.

Dotsie had a clever way to get me to clean the house. She placed a note on my bed telling me to clean the bathroom and then get my reward, on the kitchen table. After cleaning and replacing the towels in the bath, I'd go to the kitchen and find a small toy or a piece of gum, with a note: wash the dishes, then go look under your pillow. I'd wash the dishes, then go back to the bedroom to find a piece of chocolate under my pillow. With a note, of course: pick up your clothes and toys and put them all away, then go look in the oven. In the oven I'd find another toy or candy. On and on this game would play out until I had cleaned every room (to my ability) and earned every small reward. Clever.

My feelings about her were mixed, however, so even though I was just 5 when she and her buddies crept up to me one day in the backyard with a warning, I got curious instead, as if she was trying to pull my leg. She warned me to stay away from the house, because the TV repairman was there and he had "gotten to" other young girls in the neighborhood. Because I did not know exactly what she meant, I did not quite believe her, and because there were other kids in and out of our house all the time, I felt safe to investigate. There were no kids in the house. He talked me into showing him my bedroom, where he would sexually abuse me three separate times before Brent caught him and told Mother. Next thing I knew there was a policeman in the house. I was desperate for some comfort from my mother, but Dotsie told me not to go near her, because the man would ask me questions. I went anyway. I answered "no" to all the policeman's questions. My mother and I walked him down to his car. Finally, with him gone I could cry and tell my mother the truth. She was comforting and kind. The man who had "gotten to me" was developmentally disabled, and I don't believe there were any real consequences for him in this or other incidents.

When I was about 18, I got pregnant by what we called at the time, a "date rape." I carried the baby to term, and had decided to give it up for adoption. While convalescing from the birth, Dotsie told me that under no circumstances should I hold my baby, and "fergodsakes don't nurse him. You will never be able to give him up if you do." I heeded her advice this time, and regretted it for many years after. I met my son when he was 35, and I was able to apologize to him for my lack of courage, and to tell him that his grandmother had done what I could not. Well, not the nursing bit…but she came every day to the place where I was convalescing to see him and me. On the way in to my room, and on the way out again, she picked up her grandson, held him and talked to him, told him about us and told him we would never forget him.

The Dotsie-damage in me had been done long ago: to my confidence, and to my trust in Dotsie as well as in myself. I had seen other girls holding and nursing their babies. Our hearts were broken, and not likely to be less so if we did not hold our babies. Dotsie was so sure of herself, and so much an authority in my life, and at the time I was so scared, I couldn't *not* do what she said. My own doubts were too heavy.

My sister consistently and openly regarded me as her "baby sister" and treated me alternately like a child-imbecile or a peer and confidant, well into my 50's. She never sought to understand what I did in the world and the spiritual path I created for my own growth and awareness. She seemed to prefer her own understanding and perceptions about my life. I found it difficult to inject any new thoughts or possibilities with Dotsie. Rather, I think she preferred to remain in a big sister position, not wanting to accept that I had become my own self and was doing ok.

For me, developing a spiritual practice and a spirituality-based professional practice, helped me grow from my past unhealthy family dynamic. My practice allowed for me to develop confidence while I learned more deeply about my life and what powered my sense of self. I learned to apply principles and methods of healing while accepting my fears and flaws. I think Dotsie appreciated that I studied and provided healing through my practice, but had no real interest in knowing what that was about for me. Again, she seemed to prefer, and stay with, her own ideas about me and what I did in the world.

I, however, was deeply impressed to learn that my learned sister was a psychopomp. It's an old-fashioned term that means she helped people cross over, after their death, into their next level. She did it in her sleep and dreams, and had likely done this service most of her life. She told me about this unusual occupation only once, confided in me, I think. She did not swear me to secrecy but I do not believe she would have wanted it widely known, nor that she had seen some ghosts of our ancestors. She was a scientist, and scientists are not supposed to have these odd spiritual experiences.

I used to say my sister was judge, jury, and executioner in our family. There was a large grain of truth there. She remained, likely until the day she died, our mother's harshest critic. She loathed seeing Mother drinking, gesticulating wildly and slurring her words, yet still assumed the "adult" when drunk. She was the first to set a boundary for our mother, by telling her not to call if she had been drinking. That piece of modeling would lead me to set some boundaries for Mother later in my own life.

Though Dotsie was much more of a grownup than my mother ever was, and she knew it, she never was one for self-investigation. While her daughter, Emily, was in and out of detox and rehab centers, she had to attend AA and Al-Anon. It is likely that my sister went to a couple of Al-Anon meetings, too. It is also likely she quickly grew bored or at least disinterested in the central idea of Al-Anon: to work on your*self*, to focus healing and recovery in your own backyard.

I remember one time, while visiting my sister, she had injured her back. I offered a little gentle massage and promised not to work around where the pain was. She was very protective, but agreed, because maybe it would help. When I put my hands on her, her body felt like a brick. I considered for a moment whether it was because she was in pain. So, I moved to an area far from the pain and laid my hands down once again. Hard as a rock. Armored, as one of my colleagues would put it. Armored. Ok. I breathed and waited and got soft inside. She remained armored. The tissue that does that is not muscle, it is *fascia*, connective tissue that exists at every level of organization in the body, from cell to skin. Fascia supports the nervous, circulatory and lymphatic systems. It is a "thinking/experiencing" tissue. My specialty is working with fascia, so I waited, warmed, relaxed inside, messaged the fascia at a distance from her back. No deal. Even a person with active PTSD armoring, relents after a few minutes. I realized this is how my sister lives in her body: armored, defended, hardened. Armoring the body is an outgrowth of an inner attitude that one cannot appear weak, one must hide all uncertainty, even from oneself. Her rigidity in attitude had informed her body tissues to hold, close, defend. Now I am beginning to understand her childhood, her pain and suffering, her need to hold rigidly to her position of power, lest all be lost.

Our mother had much to teach to us about sobriety and recovery. Dotsie seemed to prefer her old perception of Mother, weak and diseased. Emily had much to teach us about the treachery of addiction and denial. Her own father, an alcoholic in recovery for 45 years until his death, told me he had never met a person who worked so hard to stay sober as his daughter, Emily. Dotsie's denial did not allow her to listen deeply to Emily or her sister, nor did her denial allow her to see the danger she courted as a child of two alcoholics, from a long line of alcoholics, to become one herself. As I write this, I realize my greatest wish for Dotsie, was that she was scooped up or guided home by our mother and father, and her daughter.

I do not yet know the full impact for me of losing my sister, Dotsie, to alcoholism. Or, to losing her presence in my life. I do not yet know who I am without her. I knew she was dying a few days or a week in advance, and I knew it was alcohol poisoning, she was deliberately taking her life. I did not go to LA where she lived. Her husband was no help. My brother and her younger daughter attended her death. I felt no grief, no heartache, only relief for her.

I am the spiritually-oriented person in the family. In my practice, I have attended, like a mid-wife, many people who are dying. I have conducted rituals and ceremonies for most everyone in my family, from weddings to funerals. All I could do for Dotsie was to place a small altar in my garden and ask my mother and Dotsie's daughter to come get her and carry her home. Typical, for me at least, it took 3 days, and then she was gone. No grieving.

Many years ago, I made up a kind of baptism ceremony, and anointed people with sea water, to help them shed the karma of this life and prepare to step into the next. For some reason I could not think to do that for Dotsie. Today, I am trying to stay awake and aware because I don't want to overlook my own reactions and responses, or any felt-sense of grief. So far, just relief. She is no longer suffering.

We may have made some sort of peace years ago. I was driving home after being in LA for the week after Emily died. We had held a large group "share" at Dotsie's, with family and Emily's friends. Several of us held a family memorial on the beach. We visited Em's father. We tried our best to comfort Em's daughter, Lena. I was mulling it all over while rolling up the darkened "grapevine" of Interstate 5, toward home. My sister called. She was drunk, and fearing it was all her fault. She worried she had not been a very good mother to Emily, because she could not help Em to stay sober. I reassured her that she had ful-filled her task as mother, and that it was not her fault that Emily had died. Emily was on her own path, and for all we knew, had fulfilled the requirements for her life this time. Dotsie appreciated that I spoke with her this way. When we ended our conversation, I was pretty sure Dotsie had much more grieving to do. I would pray for her comfort and relief. Oddly, we rarely spoke after that.

My mother came to see me a little while after she died. I was in that liminal space between sleep and wake, and there she was, radiant and lovely. I gasped. I heard her say in my head, "It's ok, honey, I just came to tell you I'm in a new *light*." Wherever my sister is now, I trust she is in her own new light. I wish her well and happy.

Addendum: The Twelve Steps

What follows are 12 articles describing my process through the 12 Steps of Recovery. You will notice that each article begins with the wording of each step from Alcoholics Anonymous, the Big Blue Book. It is followed by a "Proactive" step, where the wording is very different.

The Proactive 12 Steps come from Serge Prengel, who has been using the 12 Steps of AA, re-imagined, for many, many years. His Proactive steps update the language, making the steps more approachable for some people. He introduces new, subtle ideas into each step, that also point to what the step truly has to offer us as spiritual beings. Serge teaches his 12 Steps to his clients, to enable them to end bad habits and begin new, good ones.

So let me tell you some of what I have learned so far:

Proactive goes to the heart of making change. Proactive means I take responsibility, I initiate change. Being proactive requires that I slow down, reflect before I act, so that my actions are more conscious, more deeply considered. I am asked to go inside and learn about, admit and accept my limitations or patterns of behavior. To go inside, I must slow down; going inside is itself a form of slowing down. Inside there can be a gentle, piece by piece dis-containing or dissolving of my patterns and the fears that gave rise to those patterns. Inside, I am whole.

I have learned to be patient and build a tolerance for my own pain, rather than denying it or by becoming unconscious. Slowly, I have gained acceptance for who I am. Through acceptance I am learning to trust myself, and trust allows compassion to be felt. Trust and compassion for myself has led to my feeling true compassion for others.

I have learned that inside I am a theatre company of parts. Inside, I have observers, critics, scared children, mothers, teachers, managers, and protectors. Observers can sometimes be stern; an observer might wear a valence of teacher, manager or critic. The Observer in me is learning, with me, to become less critical and more curious.

I have learned to support the Observer being more "user friendly" by naming my own feelings. Identifying my feelings allows me to be the "adult in the room" inside myself. In this way, naming helps me to be less self-conscious, more self-*aware*. My inner Observer becomes a flashlight holder.

I have learned, through working the 12 Steps and the Proactive steps, to bring my new skills into my relationships—my marriage being the closest and most important at hand. Slowing down, pausing, turning inward toward the felt senses in my body, being open and curious about myself as a living, growing creature, spirit having a human experience—all raise my self-awareness and make me a better communicator, a better listening, a better partner.

These following 12 essays are my Twelve Steps. Recently, I worked with Serge Prengel, Therapist and Focuser, to delve into the classical 12 Steps of AA, and to contrast them with Serge's *Proactive 12 Steps*. With each step, we engaged in a bit of Focusing to sense their resonance in my body.

Focusing is a well-researched practice, first "discovered" by people like Carl Rogers, but deeply understood and refined by Gene Gendlin. Gene was interested in why some people seemed to really benefit from therapy, got well, so to speak, while some did not. He listened to hundreds of hours of therapy tapes and made an amazing discovery. Some people actually went inside themselves for answers. Sometimes they would say to their therapist, "Wait a minute. There is something here." They would sit quietly for a moment, then go on to describe a physical feeling, say, a *pressure*, then add an "as if" statement, such as "the world bearing down on me." That would inevitably lead to acknowledging an emotion, such as overwhelm, fear, wariness and so on. People were finding and describing, within their bodies, a *felt-sense.*

In these essays, I explore the steps in my own Focusing-like process. I include them here to demonstrate the power of the steps, even re-interpreted steps, for coming to an understanding about myself and for looking deeply into how my body holds the story and the *sense* of myself, especially when I'm under stress, and sensing my enmeshment with another. Focusing is not therapy, per se, but it is a highly therapeutic practice. Focusing leaves me feeling open and smart, I've discovered something about *me.* Sitting with my discoveries, my feelings arising around them are allowed to change, to soften, to deepen. Other feelings emerge: appreciation and gratitude, compassion and empathy.

An important aspect of Focusing, is to do it with a partner, so you can feel heard. People trained in Focusing are also trained to be deep listeners, feeding back not just the ideas you express but their own felt-sense of what it might mean, and how and where else you might look for new discoveries.

For more information and to find a teacher, consult Focusing International online.

Serge's 12 Steps also make the steps more inclusive, in that they do not include the word God or He. You can find many iterations of

Serge's Proactive 12 steps at his website: *www.proactivechange.com.*

Angel's 12 Steps

Step 1: We admitted we were powerless over alcohol—that our lives had become unmanageable.

Proactive Step 1: There is a big difference between what I do and how I want to be. I am stuck in what I do.

It is helpful to me to admit to some aspect of life being unmanageable. It is not my history or conditioning to do so, but I have learned to admit other possible options, and this is one: I am stuck in what I do. My current level of understanding cannot rectify or resolve the difference between what I do and how I want to be. This admission awakens me to a *realization* that I am not free or able to move forward. I have often "hit" this sort of "wall" before in my life, usually because I have run out of history and information that might be applied to the predicament or situation I am in. I have run out of "fixes" for this one. I am frustrated and feeling stuck, and there have been many times I fought against similar frustration by resorting to old, patterned behaviors: anger, unconsciousness, struggle, displaced responsibility, substance use.

Going inside I can feel that *stuck* feels stopped, frozen. I am not open, and am pushing or struggling against some aspect of life, trying to make *it* move. My belly tightens as I sense a need to change *it*, move *it*. And, the need to change or fix blinds me to the pattern I have fallen into. The more I struggle *against*, the smaller my perspective becomes, the narrower my vision, and the tighter my body feels.

I contract down into my belly, to the size of my predicament as my true reality. My whole body attitude is serious, tight, pulled down, yet some part of me seems rigidly determined to break through, head first, to make this frustrating discomfort go away.

Seeing, admitting that I am stuck is both an awakening and an unhappy realization. Unhappy, because my "nose to the grindstone" attitude puts unreasonable and unkind pressure on me to fix and relieve pain, move on. If I do not activate feelings of false power to handle or control the situation, I feel disloyal to my upbringing and conditioning.

At the same time the *awareness* of my pattern provides a sense there may be some part of me that is *not* caught in what I perceive my experience to be. Admitting my stuck-ness, allows for the possibility of a part of me that does not exist *within* my predicament, not imprisoned by what I feel, to also be present. Who is it that is seeing and admitting this truth? That's the one, right there, the one who is not stuck but can see the stuck-ness. An Observer.

Giving up or admitting to powerlessness or stuck-ness opens me. I feel freed to admit defeat. My body opens more, relaxes, head and chest rise, my vision expands. In my stuck and struggling mode, I am just powerless and yet I struggle. Madness. With my chest open and head perched comfortably on my spine, I can see and sense that, yes, I am powerless over that situation, but that's not the whole of who I am. In my stuck mode, I am contracted into a small, light-deprived sense of self and I am not who I want to be. As I give up, I unfold from my contraction, expand a little, light and air return, other possibilities become, well, possible.

I am reminded that I may never gain control over that particular situation. I can admit this possibility without it being a personal indictment of my lack of something. My powerlessness is actually be-ginning to feel reasonable, normal.

Knowing I am powerless allows me to feel nearer the middle of some spectrum where there is more space. I am not clinging to an extreme position, nor bouncing from one end to another. This gain in perspective humbles me. I feel softer inside and I am reminded that another word for humble is *teachable*.

Step 2: Came to believe that a Power greater than ourselves could restore us to sanity.

Proactive Step 2: I understand that I cannot force change through willpower. I need to disentangle my life patiently.

When I think of Step 1 and my realization that I am powerless and stuck somewhere in my life, I know it is because I have run out of ideas. My desire to fix the situation rather than seek to understand it, exhausts all my inherited tools—there is nothing behind me that will add to the situation, or open it, let alone get it moving again.

Step 2 points to the glimmer of something seen when exploring Step 1: specifically, there is some part of me that is *not* stuck, some aspect of consciousness that is above or outside my stuck predicament, helping me to look at it and see my stuck-ness. It is not connected to stuck-ness or powerlessness, it simply observes me in my predicament.

Engaging with Step 2, I feel that glimmer grow into a possibility. When I sit with this glimmer my head is lifted out of the "row" I am "hoeing" and I sniff something new on the wind, somewhere near. I am challenged to stretch my limited beliefs into this greater possibility, one that is at first too large to wrap my current self-understanding around. It feels like stepping into too large shoes. I want it, am intrigued, but I am uncomfortable, walking in these shoes is awkward and sloppy.

The Observer part of me seems to have access to this greater space, greater power. I follow this inkling further inward. The Observer knows, and now I am onto, I am more than stuck and powerless and I am more than my small, scared self; I am more than my history that cannot account for a "power greater than me". If I can just stand up into this "greater than" skin, I can begin to accommodate this "greater than" power.

Sitting inside I feel challenged, and at the same time invited out of my small existence into a larger world where there is a heart-lifting feeling. This sense of the larger, more open, space helps me get comfortable with being uncomfortable, out of my depth. *Coming to believe* is not easy, I think it will take time for me to fully embrace this larger field of experience. But it feels like hope, rather than powerlessness.

All of my "nose to the grindstone" beliefs and conditioning are useless here, but I also don't need to waste energy trying to cast out any of my old patterns. This feels more like an invitation to "rise above" them. "Came to believe in a power greater than myself" is like a newly adopted belief because I have lifted my nose off my particular grindstone, and I can sense and smell and feel the spaciousness to think differently. I think I'll take this one out for a test drive…

Step 3: Made a decision to turn our will and our lives over to God, as we understood Him.

Proactive Step 3: To find myself, moment by moment, I take a mindful pause to deal with my life calmly and effectively.

"Pause" from AA slogans: **Pause And Use Spiritual Energy**

Step 2 leads me to taking Step 3, which invites me to turn over my predicament, worry, or unresolvable issues to a power greater than myself. But without having recognized the *possibility* of a power greater than myself *first*, I cannot take this step of surrender. Coming to recognize there is a power greater than my small, scared self helps me remember I am *not* my problems, I am not my predicament. I am more than my patterns. More than my small, scared self.

Steps 2 and 3 invite me to discover and determine what it is I am turning over or surrendering *to*. What do I believe about this greater power? Since the God of my childhood is no longer relevant in my life, and offers no comfort, what *is* relevant? I must go inside to discover who or what this power is to me.

Taking a mindful pause, I go inside. I feel myself drop in, down in. As I come more fully into my body, I feel myself expand. Ah, I *am* more than my body, I *am* spacious and aware. I seem to sit up taller inside. I feel my energy extending, like awareness and sensitivity, radiating from within to outside my body. I feel enlarged.

As I acknowledge my larger self—body and energy—I feel a shift in my "vibration" as if the whole of my energy clarifies and brightens up a little. Expanding my sense of self and raising my energy, gives me space to sense and feel into my large S self, my Whole Self. Remembering my Whole Self is unconditionally loving and wise, enables me to be calm and kind. This Self contains, even welcomes, all my smaller willful selves to be here, too.

Feeling whole and present, with my energy right where I am, I can sense the exact *who* to turn over my insoluble problems to: my Whole Self. Because I often feel in a state of Grace when sitting this way, I simply call her "Grace." Sometimes I hear myself say, "Grace be with me today; Grace be with me in this love thing; Grace be with me with this person" (especially when I am counseling someone). Going inside this way, finding Grace and sitting with my Whole Self is a mindful pause. Grace is waiting to receive what I cannot carry alone.

Step 3 feels like a move toward sanity and away from my *insanity* of isolation, willfulness, judging, needing to be right, and doing the same behaviors over and over again without changing the results. Sanity feels open and loving, a relief from having to know it all or be it all, practicing awareness over self-consciousness, being transparent to myself and with others. Taking a mindful pause stops me from my tendency to keep pushing mindlessly. The power of Step 3 is in the *deciding* to move toward life, toward light, toward movement and healthier self-concepts. The power of taking that mindful pause is that it enables me to be embodied, to feel power within and to return to the world of possibility.

A story: My daughter, who lived in L.A. with her husband, had a baby girl, Lauren. I attended the birth, and stayed a few days to help out. My daughter's husband seemed very stressed and protective of the baby and of my daughter. I told them that I had decided to go home to San Francisco, and to come back in one week, to help out with the baby, meals and housework. My daughter liked the idea. When I came back one week later, they were gone. No note, no call, an empty apartment. I could not get my daughter to answer her phone. I worried all the way back to San Francisco.

I learned that my son-in-law was psychologically unstable, mentally ill. He had persuaded my daughter to go to Colorado, to his family home, but not to tell her own family about the journey. I could not get in touch with her because he had taken her phone. When I called the family home, I was told that I was a horrible person and would not be able to speak to my daughter.

My daughter's father and I considered many options: lawyers, police, showing up at the house in Colorado. After many attempts to contact my daughter, her father and I decided to pull back, do nothing for the time being, give the situation, and my daughter, time to come forward. We thought there was nothing that could keep her from us for long.

But, I could not let go of the worry about her health and safety, the anger I felt toward her husband and his family, and my powerlessness over the whole situation. I needed to find a way to move on, to re-focus on my life and my young son.

One day I felt desperate to do something about my daughter and her situation. I looked around my room to see if anything might inspire me. I noticed the Bible among my other books. Ordinarily it would not have occurred to me to read the Bible, but this was not an ordinary time and I felt I needed a non-ordinary solution. I opened the book to a random page. My eyes fell on 1 Corinthians 13, where Paul talks about the power of love. I thought: maybe this is something I can *do*.

If I speak in the tongues of mortals and of angels, but do not have love, I am a noisy gong or a clanging cymbal. And if I have prophetic powers, and understand all mysteries and all knowledge, and if I have all faith, so as to remove mountains, but do not have love, I am nothing. If I give away all my possessions, and if I hand over my body so that I may boast, but do not have love, I gain nothing.

Love is patient; love is kind; love is not envious or boastful or arrogant or rude. It does not insist on its own way; it is not irritable or resentful; it does not rejoice in wrongdoing, but rejoices in the truth. It bears all things, believes all things, hopes all things, endures all things."

The very first day I offered this "prayer" for my daughter, an amazing feeling came over me. I could feel, physically, a dark weight lifting from my body, from my heart and up and out the top of my head. I felt that Grace had lifted this burden from me, I was giving it up to a greater power. I decided to pray for my daughter every day for 30 days, and sometimes twice per day. I sat quietly, read this passage to myself, and offered it to my daughter. It was my way of protecting her, and being in a state of love so I could send love. Doing this everyday freed me to grieve and to let go. It also enabled me to move back into my life and responsibilities with greater ease.

After five years, my daughter and I re-united in joy. There were questions but no recriminations, no guilt or judgment.

"Love never ends. But as for prophecies, they will come to an end; as for tongues, they will cease; as for knowledge, it will come to an end. For we know only in part, and we prophesy only in part; but when the complete comes, the partial will come to an end.

 For now we see in a mirror, darkly, but then we will see face to face. Now I know only in part; then I will know fully, even as I have been fully known. And now faith, hope, and love abide, these three; and the greatest of these is love."
1 Cor. 13, 1-13

I still do not believe in one divine being. I believe in a divine *state* of being.

Step 4: Made a searching and fearless moral inventory of ourselves.

Proactive Step 4: Made a loving and fearless inventory of ourselves.

Step 4 encourages me to tell my positive truths and my negative truths without judgment or embellishment. It says in the AA Blue Book I should not rush to complete the task, nor procrastinate in working with it.

This step calls for an altar, I hear myself say. I will make my lists of assets and deficits and place them on an altar. An altar, in this case, is not for worshipping; rather, it is a focal point—on a window sill, a bookshelf, next to my bed or a space in the garden. I gather a few items that seem to call to me—a few stones, a feather, a ceramic animal, beads—personal objects are gathered for the purpose of creating a little sacred space, a meeting place for me and my Higher Power, a place for my inventory to rest.

The Big Blue AA Book, suggests beginning with my assets, and I can sense the wisdom in this advice. If I start with my deficits, I'll get focused there and might be able to find only 4 or 5 assets. Beginning with my assets, I start the process with a longer list.

Taking my inventory includes listing *potentials*, skin deep, underdeveloped aspects of myself that have not yet come to full corpus, perhaps a direction I am *aimed* toward. Including potentials feels right even though I am not yet aware of what they are or might be.

My partner and I sit together, meditate for a few minutes, and drop into our bodies more deeply. As I drop in I can sense many word-ideas clamoring for my attention. I breathe a little more, stalling for time, making sure these words are not only in my head. Breathing, I calm inside, beginning to feel more centered as well as embodied. In the center of myself I sense I'm in a garden, an apple tree and other fruits surround me. I pick an apple and it "says" to me *generous*. I am generous. Another pick feels like love to me, and I sense it is the *knowledge* of love, I can love and *be* loved. I care about people, animals, earth, I am learning to listen with compassion... And on it goes until I have a pretty impressive list of assets.

My partner and I compare our lists. We add assets to each other's lists as well. We place our lists on our respective altars. Since doing so I have felt inspired to go back and add a few items to my list. And, I have added water, earth, fire (candle) and nature and mineral to my altar, to allow all the attributes of being human to come to balance with the elements of earth.

Back inside to consider my other list, my deficits. Already, I feel differently about my so-called deficits. Inside, in my garden, I experience a wide variety of fruits: some blossoming potentials, some ready and in use, some rotting on the ground, spent and lifeless, some getting ready to drop. Most of these fruits of self are about how I am in relationship with others. Some of my behaviors have become useless, rotten: my defensiveness, the way I hide rather than own up to who I am; my tendency for judgment. Ready to drop and die is my fear of being vulnerable. I sense I must eat this overripe apple, digest its meaning and history, to really let it go. Seeing and sensing my deficits in this way somehow neutralizes them just enough to make them ready to pluck, they are less charged and I am appropriately distant yet compassionate, I can be differently in *relation* to my deficits.

One of my 4th step deficits is to interrupt my listening to another by trying to fix his problem. Fixing is not listening. But I have a habit of jumping into solution mode when my partner is describing his personal experience. When I do this, I can feel him close up. I lose his trust because he can tell I am not really listening, and rapport between us suffers a setback. It's a deeply engrained pattern in me and when I engage with this pattern I feel my need to avoid pain and suffering, to make myself useful, and to distract him from his experience.

It is risky to be open with another—to be vulnerable and transparent. And, I can be busy inside myself, waiting to butt in, attempting to solve problems. My fear of listening to my partner's pain only serves to minimize his internal experience, making it less important than the solution I offer.

Imagine carrying the weight of an internal dilemma for many years, the fear that you will not be sufficiently heard, for instance, and risking being vulnerable anyway. Imagine, I come along with a way to distract you from being with your fear, to shift the conversation towards a solution, and basically show you how silly you are for carrying that fear all your life, don't you know how easy it is to fix?

I feel ashamed of my pattern and I can sense how maddening and insulting my behavior is to others. So now it is my task to sit with this shame in a compassionate way, wait, and listen for what it has to teach me. The story is: This pattern and others, helped me to survive in my family, to get along, and look as if I care about the other, while inside I line up fixes for the other to try. Beneath or inside this pattern is a small me, desperate to find a way to help my alcoholic mother come back to me, be with me. If I can help her, I won't have to live the pain and confusion of her being gone and in the room with me at the same time. Without doing this pattern, I am not sure that I will be able to listen well, and I am unsure of what my role could or should be, so I, too, am "gone". More sitting with…

Meanwhile, on the altar, time is suspended. My lists cook in the belly of my higher power, Grace, who, like nature, works largely unseen miracles and carries a bigger shovel than I. Like laying down a basket of heavy rocks, I feel freed up, restored to a state of becoming, a grower and transformer, no longer a hauler or hoarder. Alchemy happens when I turn my list over to my Higher Power, a higher or clearer consciousness. When I come back to my list, much of what was charged and painful no longer has the power it seemed to have.

Step 5: Admitted to God, to ourselves, and to another human being the exact nature of our wrongs.

Proactive Step 5: I explore these patterns and describe them to another person, noticing the shame I feel but also the healing power of compassionate listening.

Step 5 is an antidote for secrecy and hiding in the family. As a child of alcoholic parents, I learned to bond to my family through the family agreement to keep quiet about the dysfunctional elephant in the middle of the room. I gained membership in the family through secrets, desperate to hold and maintain my place within the family system. From that point of view, it feels dangerous and disloyal to tell the emperor he isn't wearing any clothes.

In Step 5 I tell my story, my truth, to Grace and another human being. I break the old bond of silence and secrecy, making myself transparent and vulnerable. The risk of full disclosure is to stir the great sea of **shame**. As painful as it is to bare my soul, however, it is also liberating.

Shame: In my mind, a damning, a judgment; my survival is threatened, the clan will throw me out. It threatens to crush me into nothing; I am exposed in my behavior and flawed-ness. In my body I feel somehow wrong to my core, compressed down into a very small self; hotly humiliated.

The only antidotes I know of to the power of shame is (1) what might be called *exposure therapy*: Al-anon meetings are like exposure therapy—every week I get a dose of transparency and nothing happens except I am accepted and listened to; and (2) forgiveness. I continue to attend Al-anon, because with all my flaws and deficits, I can feel normal in a room with others like me. Eventually I came to trust my ability to open and handle my pain with others.

I sit with one of my deficits: I don't want to expose my distress to those I love. Dropping in, and opening myself toward a felt sense, I feel a tug-o-war around my heart area. I want to tell, but am afraid of feeling shame and burdening another. The story my heart knows is of feeling misdirected and responsible. To tell my mother that I need her, am anxious when she drinks and leaves me behind, threatens to add to *her* misery, *her* burden. And my role with her, as I see it from my very young self, is to take care of *her*, so she can, hopefully, take care of me. My stomach reports an uncomfortable sort of fullness. Ah, it seems I eat my anxiety rather than share it. I chew on the inside of my cheek and bite my nails. It doesn't really rid me of anxiety, only keeps me busy doing something with the energy of distress.

The energy of distress abducts my attention outwardly. Already feeling or fearing abandonment by my mother, I abandon my*self* and add to my distress by obsessing on what I can do for *her* so she will be freed up to comfort *me*. All this activity and outward focus distracts me from the feeling of being utterly powerless to affect my life. This pattern of helplessness has been pumping out anxiety for many, many years now.

I sit close to my small, abandoned and anxious self until she is calm and still. I tell her that I must, as part of the healing for us both, lay our stories out to another human being, and place our stories on my altar for my Higher Power, Grace, to aid the digestion process. In doing so I promise to lighten her load, and mine. I let her know she is not alone, I will be with her now.

Step 6: Were entirely ready to have God remove all these defects of character

Proactive Step 6: I understand how these patterns have been ways of coping with my fears. (And I share this understanding with the god of my heart, my Higher Power, Grace).

Taking Step 6 seems to require my deeper attention. Am I ready to surrender my "defects" or deficits? Am I ready to unravel my patterns, knowing that they are tethered to other parts of me, my beliefs and perspectives? My okay patterns of thought and relating may be intertwined with my unwanted patterns of thought and relating, so to pull out one strand of my woven insides, could unravel many aspects of my self—am I ready to do that?

For instance, my ingrained pattern of fixing interferes with careful listening to my partner. My activation of this pattern of wanting to help him fix what is inside him, is well known now to both of us. In deeper conversation we are both wary—I'm afraid of not being useful or insightful for him, he is worried I will *try* to be useful and stop his inner process. But, it's good to be helpful, right?

I can hear how caught I have become in my fear of change. My fears helped me create patterns to control, avoid and defend myself in the first place—perhaps I should be more willing to make this change. But here I am trying to *control* the rate of change within me, wanting to *avoid* upsetting the apple cart of my life, and *defending* my hesitation by questioning my readiness. I need a new influx of information and possibility to work with my patterns. Time to pause, get quiet, and sense into my fears.

I go inside. My habit is to say hello to myself, to re-orient myself to my insides, and to open to my whole-self presence. I ask for help from Grace, my Higher Power. My attention is drawn to a space between my belly and my heart. Tightness. Another tug-o-war between my inner centers of power as I seek to engage with the requirements of this step. I listen to the conflict and sense it is between the part of me that wants to control, hold on, not give up too fast, and the part of me that holds a higher truth about my patterns, and is ready for change. It is pretty clear that the part of me that has a tight hold and wants to control the unfolding of events, is fearful of change, fearful of change that I do not consciously walk into, fearful of what else will change if I let go, as if my entire life will unravel, all the strands will come loose at once.

Nothing for it but to sit some more and breathe, wait.

Tribal fears: not being useful is considered disloyal in my tribe (family). *Deciding* to not be useful pulls the rug out from under one of my primary functions in the world, and feels like I am threatening to remove a major part of who I think I am, that I also admire. A trap door on the floor of my body opens and a few ideas slither out: motivation for being useful or helping is skewed, smells of control vs genuine helping. If I can help, "we" can avoid pain, because my helping can distract from pain, and I am seen as a person of great value. Oh, it's about me and feeling valuable or not in my family. I recall feeling so needy and helpless in my childhood with my alcoholic, chronically depressed mother, that if there was any one small thing I could do, it might help, and my mother would be so relieved, she might perceive me as a valuable person, and she would love me. Okay, let's sit with Neediness, she looks like she could use a friend. Sitting close I feel desperately lonely, I crave simple attention and recognition. I am also afraid of too much attention coming my way. Another conflict. I back up a little.

So down here in the darkness, it's about feeling love and being seen. Well, Grace, there have to be better ways to be of help to people, ways not tied to my neediness. Ultimately, I sense I am looking to change, to eliminate Neediness' job and power, her influence within me and her tendency to inject herself into my motivations. So, I ask Grace to help me sort it all out. Be with me. Help me bring love to myself, help me see myself and reveal myself to others.

Is there anything else? Another idea slithers out from the trap door: It's also about power and powerlessness. I feel powerful when I can help someone. Helping, from this perspective, induces the other to give me positive attention. But, at bottom, I am feeling powerless most of the time, my motivation for helping is to avoid the pain of powerlessness, so this helping thing for *his* sake is not an authentic way of being with him, or with me.

Feeling amazed and slightly stunned at the depth and pervasiveness of these patterns in me, and also appreciating their origins, I am ready to surrender. And, excited to surrender these the fears that have supported their own existence for so long, I feel ready to turn them over and welcome a new phase of learning.

Step 7: Humbly asked God to remove our shortcomings.

Proactive Step 7: I learn to accept the sense of vulnerability that goes with life's pressures and uncertainties.

Another word for humble is *teachable*. To say "I humbly asked God" implies I am open, willing to learn, curious. The proactive step also implies that I am open—open to learn, open to accept, and perhaps more open to be with myself *in* my vulnerability. This step brings me a little closer to the heart of my pattern: I need to learn a new way to be inside by building a tolerance for my discomfort and allowing my tolerance to grow into an easier self-acceptance.

Real growth and evolution comes not just from shedding the old, but from learning and integrating new, *healthier* ways of being with myself and others. My brain has taken a long time to learn my old patterns, make neuronal pathways to gather all the associations I need to activate my patterns, including all the short cuts that speedily bring me to the emotional content and charge associated with my pattern, effectively by-passing the thinking process.

Going inside to learn about, to admit and and accept my pattern, requires time. Growth requires time. Changing a pattern requires time and trust, and a bit of education plus new skill building and practicing until the new skills are integrated and my brain creates a neuronal pathway to help them feel normal.

Inside, I sit with my anger, my fury. Anger makes me feel larger and less vulnerable, which provides a big hint about what fuels this kind of anger: fear and vulnerability. Anger has often felt overwhelming to me so I can see and sense inside a part of me that rigidly holds whatever position I have taken up with the other. This rigidity helps me manage my desire to run away, the rigidity is both a way to gain control and a reaction to feeling I have lost all control.

It's very uncomfortable in my body. There is tension, tightness and contraction in my chest and gut. Under the tension of my anger is the perception of hurt, the deep pain of rejection and feeling criticized instead of understood. I feel myself want to hit out or hit back, bite like a wild animal, and immediately feel shame for wanting to punish the other. The variety and intensity of feelings overwhelms me, and I sit in confusion. Then I sit *with* confusion and overwhelm. Slowly I seem to regain a sense of equilibrium, and the excited, angry/hurt feelings subside. My breathing slows and I realize I have been *in* my pattern, not just observing it.

A deeper truth slowly emerges: This pattern needs the attention of my higher power, Grace, who will consider the whole of the pattern from a higher vibration or higher level of thought. Turning it over, I am relieved of some of the charge of the pattern and I feel more capable of knowing and understanding my pattern with anger, dis-containing it a piece at a time. I feel ready to engage in a learning process. As much as I want to release the pattern and be done with it, it feels more right to *accept* the pattern as a creation designed to keep me safe. I will continue to sit with myself to build my ability to tolerate emotions linked to old experiences, while I learn to accept the sense of vulnerability as a fact of my humanity.

Turning over this experience, I am reminded that change, real change, is a long process, a journey through layers of experience and perception that requires building a *tolerance* for my hurting self and patterns, becoming *accepting* of my hurting self and patterns. Consider sailing. If the boat is large like my entrenched patterns, turning the wheel to change course will move the rudder, the underwater, unconscious aspect of me holding the pattern. But, if you have sailed, you know it requires a little time for the boat to come around to its new course. The larger the boat, the more time is required to come about, to come to the new direction.

An injured, angry, unaccepting me wants a quick fix—just make it go away. But this pattern is attached to so much inside me that it needs to be teased gently out, all of its' strands pulled, replaced by new thoughts, new understandings and new behaviors. Real change and growth takes time. Accepting and admitting my vulnerability is a humbling and valuable first step.

Step 8: Made a list of all persons we had harmed, and became willing to make amends to them all.

Proactive Step 8: I explore alternative behaviors and rehearse them in safe settings.

My list of harms is clear to me: fixing instead of listening, lying, avoiding, protecting and defending, failing to show up, lack of transparency. And, I can acknowledge how my behaviors affected other people: my partners, my kids, my parents, my friends, my siblings, and myself.

When I don't fully show up for my present partner, when I defend my apparent behavior instead of listening to the affect my behavior has had upon him, I can feel myself get smaller inside. I am guarding and protecting this small, hurt self, and my victim perspective. I rigidly stand behind my behavior, finding other possible reasons for it to *appear* to offend my partner. I am not listening, I am defending.

Since making my lists of positive and negative traits (my Step 4 inventory), and asking my Higher Power, Grace, for help and strength, it has become easier to acknowledge my behaviors toward others and to apply the part of the prayer for **Serenity to accept what cannot be changed**. I cannot change my childhood, I cannot change harm already done.

Finding **Courage to change what I can** will enable me to make amends to others and myself, to dedicate myself to making my new, healthy behaviors more stable and reliable, and to admit when I fail to meet these higher standards.

I feel I have and can call in **Wisdom to know the difference** that is largely the wisdom to recognize when I am in an active pattern and hiding behind the need for protection. Wisdom then becomes knowing my patterns also need the attention of my higher power, Grace, who will consider the whole of the pattern from a higher vibration or higher level of thought.

I go inside. I breathe, relax and settle in. Sitting with my pattern of self-defense, I can sense me leaping to a conclusion that I am one kind of *self,* rigid and inflexible, and am a slave to this persona or part. I must obey. Being defensive comes out of this rigidity. This part of me is highly identified with survival. Seeing and sensing into the truth of how I am *in* my pattern makes room for the real thing I am learning about to emerge: to acknowledge and let go of the *self-image* that helps me perpetuate the dominance of this part, and all its behaviors. Sitting with and listening to this self-image seems to help *make room* inside and soften who I have been; I can begin experimenting with a more flexible self. I see that I can learn, by practice, to let go of or really diminish the influence of this rigid self. I can employ new behaviors, new tools to replace my identification with this old, small victim self.

It is important not to speed up around these revelations. Rather, I slow enough to feel where I am and who I am trying to be or not be. Out of my inner self I see the new behaviors to help manage this change in self-image: **slow down, pause and visit my interior self.**

Time seems an important factor. I could *ask* for time! My partner will give time if I ask for it. My new pattern can look like this: slow down, pause, go inside, find courage to ask. I can tolerate feeling vulnerable. My partner is a safe person to practice with. I am already learning, through practice, to "put down the gun" of my excited self and pick up the courage to be patient and transparent. Now I can ask for time if I need it.

I not only identify a new behavior (slow down, pause, ask) but also practice in a safe setting: I slow down with my partner, I trust his openness, I ask for what I need and do what he does: go inside and listen. These new behaviors will enable me to not only identify where and to whom I need to make amends, but will serve to ground me and enable me to be more present while I do it.

Step 9: Made direct amends to such people wherever possible, except when to do so would injure them or others.

Proactive Step 9: I apply these new mindful behaviors in my everyday life. I sincerely apologize to people I have hurt, except when it would be counterproductive to do so.

Making amends provides a shift in energy state for myself and those I have injured. For me, I clear guilt and regret, as well as *shame*, one of the most toxic emotions. Making amends to another makes space in me for *self*-forgiveness. I hope what I offer to the injured party will shift them to a cleaner, clearer energy state, where they can let go of any harbored emotions, such as resentment.

Making amends for old hurts is humbling: I must be transparent, direct, and ask for but not expect the offended party to forgive me, or even to bear with me and my behavior. I must admit my wrongdoing. To do this is humbling but I sense also liberating.

Admitting my wrong and apologizing *in the moment* is a new behavior, often hard for me to do. It requires that I slow down inside, stop rushing to defend myself. It requires that I let go of who is right or wrong, and simply deal with the others' *perception* of hurt my behavior has caused. It requires that I acknowledge but put aside my tendency to fix, justify, deny, defend, or explain myself in any way.

My husband became pretty seriously ill. Our priorities have rearranged themselves around his illness. Lately when I do something that causes injury, or the perception of hurt in the moment, I quickly realize my old tendencies of fixing and defending are no longer important. Those old behaviors seem to move aside quickly, making way for easier, sincere apologies. It is a strange way to loosen my old patterns of self-defense, but I accept the help I am receiving from our new priorities because I become quickly aware of my feelings and the truth of our predicament all at once. I listen better, and am able to accept even the *perception of hurt* as a legitimate cause for my full attention and acknowledgment.

I asked my wise husband if he would be open to hearing my amends, if he were my ex-husband. He suggested that I invite my ex-husband to be part of my making amends, and then leave the ball in his court. I think it's a great idea and so composed an email to my ex asking him to meet with me. He needs time, and that gives me time to prepare myself.

I go inside. I open a pocket of regret, lodged between my heart and my belly. Most of what I sense inside this pocket is old stories, old messes in relationships: my ways of withholding attention and listening from my kids, pre-occupation with men and career, and dishonesty, or at least lack of transparency with others, money worries or the way my decisions were shaped by money.

In these old, past relationships, I seemed to not be able to find the truth of my own experience, let alone express it to my partners. I caused confusion and pain, and ran away from confrontations. I cheated and lied.

Amends, I sense, must also be made to myself, for I have injured myself many times over, in and out of relationships. I have avoided and lied to myself, abandoned myself, aligned with dodgy people, given up my power to men and women, not stood up for myself (being defensive is not the same as standing up for myself). I often failed to protect myself from harm. By not protecting myself, I put my kids at risk as well.

How will I make amends to myself? When I ask the question inside, I see the image of my list of deficits on my altar. It seems like a natural first step—add my errors and injuries to my list, and return it to the altar where the list can "cook" with spirit and my Higher Power, Grace. In other words, first, give it up.

Next, it seems I must seek a deeper understanding of where all this past behavior has come from. Not just the childhood stories and injuries I received, but the beliefs I formed from those experiences.

Life is dangerous, a mine field. Be wary and keep your distance.

I am unlovable. No one really cares.

I am abandoned, left to figure it out and fend for myself.

One part of me judges, another part of me manages my energy and responses. I see and sense how hard it has been most of my life to dig down to the authentic in me. Some smaller, well defended me has been guarding my authenticity so well, that it can't always be easily accessed.

I sit with this idea. I wait.

I have to protect what is good about me, my essence, my nature, and anything that might be regarded as special.

I am anxious.

I care more deeply than even I know.

I am capable of fierceness.

It is my true nature not to hurt, not to offend.

It is my nature to open gently, like a flower.

I usually have four paws on the ground. I like to move.

I care about your opinion of me, but I care more about *my* opinion of me.

I am spirit having a human experience. My *name* is Angel, but I am in a human life.

Is there anything else?

I want to use my power for good.

In my human life, I have screwed up, and will occasionally screw up during the rest of my human life. Making amends is part of being human. I want to be a human who works to play well with others, to believe in herself and others, and to make corrections in direction and behavior in order to uplift and restore peace, love and harmony among people I encounter. The secret to becoming this kind of human, I sense, is slowing down. Slowing down inside is my new behavior, that helps me to pause and go inward, to access my feelings in the moment, to short circuit my tendencies to override the other with fixing, and helps me to pay full attention to the interaction I am in. I sense the process of making amends encourages me to open to the reality and pain in another, to sense into their experience of my harm. The essence of making amends is empathy.

Step 10: Continued to take personal inventory and when we were wrong promptly admitted it.

Proactive Step 10: I keep paying attention to the causes and effects of my actions. I act accordingly.

From Step 9: Admitting my wrong and apologizing *in the moment* is a new behavior, often hard for me to remember to do. It requires that I slow down inside, stop rushing to defend myself. It requires that I acknowledge but put aside my tendency to fix, justify, deny, defend, or explain myself in any way.

Also in Step 9: I seem to be a better listener; I can hear and accept the *perception of hurt* as a legitimate cause for my full attention and acknowledgment.

There is no right or wrong about perceiving a hurt. I honor my partner's inner experience when I do not try to take it away by justifying myself or denying. Slowing down inside is a recently learned behavior, one that enables me to access my feelings in the moment, and to short circuit my tendencies to override my partner with fixing—to pay full attention to the interchange I am in with him.

Paying attention in the moment is also a new habit, still in formation and stabilizing day by day as I receive opportunities to check in with myself and pay attention to my interactions. The key for me is *slowing down* which enables me to pay attention. This step is not just about promptly admitting my transgressions to the other, but also about paying attention to how I feel inside, my actions based on those feelings, and to the effect my actions have on the other.

Going inside I sense that pocket between my heart and belly is full of light. Within the light is an idea, a revelation: paying attention allows me to move closer to empathy. I feel open to understand and accept my partner's experience and pain. I feel myself move toward this revelation with a knowing that the continual use of sincere acknowledgment and amends in the moment can grow empathy in me, with life providing ample opportunity to exercise and express empathy for myself and others.

I sense again, the essence of making amends is empathy.

A little deeper I sense an action I habitually take is *reaction*. I react by contracting, by pulling away from hearing something about me that I want to get mad about rather than listen to. Paying attention to this habit, I can feel myself contract, but I have enough distance from my triggered feelings to sit with them, see them. Contracting into myself cuts me off from empathy for the other and myself.

Pulling away is akin to retracting my finger from fire, I am afraid of what the other sees in me. I think I can't handle it, so I contract into my fear, my perception of harm or injury. This is an old reaction-habit in me. It is like flinching, waiting for assault. Slow down. Slow down. Look again, sit with, get a little closer.

Again, I feel like I'm waiting for the other shoe to drop, anticipating injury. There is a story behind this reaction, but I don't need to hear the story to know its' origins and how it created in me a vigilance about being hurt—with words or in a physical way. Getting this close is a little scary, but I don't feel as if I am being pulled under, more like I am gently uncovering bandages from an old scar. Sitting with my contracting this way makes it possible for me to make friends with this pattern, and I feel immediately taller and stronger just knowing it. The fears that had me construct this defense system no longer feels as potent, the fears themselves are letting down their collective guard, and I relax.

In my belly, little blue birds assemble on a runway. They are excited, chatting, ready to take flight. Each holds a straw in its beak, a resource. When they fly together, they can build something, each adding her bit of resource. It's a sweet image, and I feel more whole, more present acknowledging I have resources. Looking back over the process of working the steps, I can see I started weakly, without resources or strengths, powerless. My only option was to be open to my lack of power, to admit to powerlessness. Now I have resources for building strength, awareness and empathy!

I become aware again of the pocket of light. Paying attention in the moment, or going inside and willingly giving attention helps build the bridge to empathy, to seeing and sensing my own or the other persons' reality and reactions to my behaviors. Somehow, being aware of the light, enables me to trust I can bring these gifts of awareness with me into relationship. Awareness, in fact, may be my greatest natural resource. I may not be perfect at slowing down, listening to myself and the other, approaching with openness, bringing attention and all the other relatively new skills, but they are with me. They are mine. Through my little "failures" I will have ample opportunity for reflection and practice in being willing to make deeply considered amends in the moment.

In "To Kill a Mockingbird" wise father, Atticus Finch, tells his precocious daughter, Scout, you never really know a person until you see things from their point of view, walk around in their shoes for a while (paraphrased). *Empathy.*

Step 11: Sought through prayer and meditation to improve our conscious contact with God, as we understood Him, praying only for knowledge of His will for us, and the power to carry that out.

Proactive Step 11: I make space in my life for mindful reflection. A sense of meaning and purpose naturally arises from that.

Step 11 feels like a natural next step, building upon all the others. I have been "working" the steps, delving into each one by listening to my inner thoughts and felt senses, so to continue to meditate and deeply consider my life and understanding through the steps seems easy. Though I do not have a "God" in my life, in the usual sense of a deity, I do have a Higher Power. Since that HP comes from my capital S self, my Whole Self, I can assume that this larger, higher vibrational part of me has a "will" or plan for my growth and evolution. I can sit in the reflection of that plan whenever I meditate, and when I include a *Metta* or loving kindness style meditation, I open my heart for hearing that plan and being in affinity with it.

Serge's proactive step reminds me that the AA call to God, even the "as we understood Him" God, is a call to reflection, a reminder to bring my attention inside, perhaps to move toward the light, toward a higher vibration of thought and a clearer state of being. To listen inside to myself as a whole being. And, by implication, to listen with openness and the capability of compassion. He suggests that having this inside relationship with myself, is a way to maintain conscious contact with God.

Serge's view on God and the 12 Steps of AA helped me to make an important distinction (page 16 of *The Proactive 12 Steps* by Serge

Prengel, 6th edition): that if you have God in your life, you have an all-powerful, all-mighty being helping you in your recovery. If you don't have a God, you still have the 12 Steps, and the real power inherent in the 12 Steps are the Steps themselves. With or without God, the 12 Steps have helped millions of people over the years and will continue to do so.

Step 11 calls me to pause often for reflection. Through working the steps, I have eliminated many obstacles to being with myself, and I have traveled inward with kindness and the capability of compassion. I am building the possibility for a real relationship with myself, and this step encourages me to continue to nurture that relationship.

And, I do not need to always be in a meditative state to slow down, pause and reflect. Perhaps I can create the habit of pausing often during the day for a short reflective time: What did I just say? What was my attitude? How do I feel about myself right now? What's going on inside right now? What affect did my behavior have just now?

I go inside to mindfully connect with myself, and to court the sense of meaning and purpose arising from my experience. In my process, I start by saying hello to myself. I use my first name. As I have shared with others for many years now, I am the most important person I will speak to all day, so it is appropriate to say hello to myself. Doing so orients me to my mind, my body and my overall presence inside. Saying hello, allows me to feel myself dropping in, settling into the bowl of my pelvis, feeling my feet, my seat and my back against the chair I sit in.

As I notice my physical self, inside, my body calms, breathing becomes deeper and more regular. I continue to say hello to anything that arises within me: a felt sense, a worry or concern, an opening or shift of consciousness, a weight I'm carrying, feeling the lifting of burdens, the rise and fall of curiosity. My hello becomes a greeting, a way to acknowledge my experience, and maintain a small distance from it at the same time. It also helps me approach with friendliness. I notice the ease of sitting inside myself. I wait. I listen. I reflect upon who I have been today among others and watch the film of my day float by, one frame at a time. I see where I have gotten excited, been triggered, been patient, laughed, wondered. These frames show me myself and how I am with others. I can sense I am conscious here, unconscious there, re-directed, shut down, or opening to life and possibilities. I sense into the reality I create inside without the need to change anything, yet often when I do sense my insides, change happens. I feel my body soften, my heart open, I feel my hardness melting, I feel joy. Some aspects of me are shifting while others are fine as they are, they simply pop up for acknowledgment.

Sometimes the best thing about meditation is having no agenda. Going in without a plan, without a question, without the need to be any different from the way I am. Just sitting with myself, feeling myself, being myself. Sitting this way, I am refreshed and renewed.

And, sometimes the best thing about meditation is having an agenda, a question, and bringing it inside with me for study. Inside, I expand and raise my vibration, inviting Grace to fill me, be with me. Grace has the whole picture. I am encouraged to see from a higher level, sense from wholeness. Meaning and purpose are sensed, the way I sense the right spot to place a puzzle piece.

Step 12: Having had a spiritual awakening as a result of these steps, we tried to carry this message to others, and to practice these principles in all our affairs.

Proactive Step 12: My life reflects a growing sense of respect and compassion for myself and others. I share this process with others who are struggling.

I am sitting in a Focusing space with my husband and his very spiritually accomplished friend, trying to assist him to contact ancestors or make connection to the other world, and ask for healing. As he describes his central dilemma, I realize I am calling in ideas to help him. Help him not hurt so much, help him see a bigger picture, help him by saying and doing the right things.

He explains—again—that he has a strong expectation, based upon his experience, that he will not be heard or seen, will not be understood. Not being heard or seen makes him suspicious about anyone trying to understand through their own filters. He wants to be seen, and will not move toward others, but will wait, insist, that someone reaches in to him.

I realize that I, too, have this same pain, and feel, as my husband, the isolation, the aloneness of not being seen, and the fear/feeling that others are just not interested to look very close to see me. Our friend has the same pain in him as well. At the same time I am full of ideas, thoughts, fix-its, and my ears are clogged with my own very old pain at my isolation and mistrust.

I begin to put aside my tools. My husband is disappointed that neither his friend nor I have given feedback that we see and hear him. So I tell him that I am sitting with my own pain in the same way he is, and I am removing obstacles to seeing and hearing him. He is not difficult to hear, as he would have it, but his candor has touched a raw nerve in me. I have spent years piling fix-its and positive platitudes on top of my pain of not being recognized, and now I am laying it bare so that I can hear him and see him directly. So I can feel what he feels.

He hears *me*, and is full of appreciation for the work I have done that has brought me to this place of being interested in his pain and his inner reality. If I go back a few steps, I can see that I have un-covered this tendency in myself to fix or want to, that I have sought to replace this habit by being with the other or myself, by investing in my inner life and by giving up this fixing tendency to Grace, my higher power, as well as asking for real insights and help to change it. All my work on the Steps has worked on me, led me to this treasure of understanding.

And here it is, his simple idea: sit with *him* so he can sit with *it*, put aside my helpful ways and means, reflect back to him how his pain has touched mine in a way that begins to clear the clutter so I can hear him better, and when appropriate, *reach* toward him with true compassion.

My spiritual awakening is to know that I am not here to be help-ful, to take away his experience so that I will be more comfortable. My spiritual awakening is to know and accept how powerless I am. My spiritual awakening is to uncover the truth in me that allows me to truly connect with him.

How do I "take this message to others?" What does it look like to "practice these principles in all our affairs"? How do you take it to others during a pandemic?

Proactive: *How* does my life reflect a growing sense of respect and compassion for myself and others? How can I share this process with others who are struggling?

Going inside I sit with my tendencies and patterns that are shifting, slowly being replaced by new, and I think, healthier ways of tuning my awareness. I see that to add "be more proactive" to my awareness means I must not only notice subtle changes in my communications with others, but comment on them: get curious, be open to what the other is experiencing. And be curious within myself to feel for the shifting tides of intimacy and caring, the in-warding and out-warding of attention that happens in relationships.

I feel odd in my own feet, as if I have shifted to firmer ground. I am quietly excited to try out these new wings, test this new freedom. Because being able to notice my tendency to fix or want to fix, in the moment, and setting it aside to really listen and be with myself or another, to get quieter and more attentive inside, is freeing. And, it no longer feels like big work.

If I had a kind of energetic meter inside, I would see evidence of growing self-respect and compassion. Inside, I simply feel freer and more open, available. I know at times I will fail to remember this new state I am cultivating, go back to my old patterns. But I can feel the compassion bank account is fairly full, so I believe I can draw out a little here and there, to help me remember to be kind to myself if there is a setback.

My **Step Sisters** (12 Step) group has met monthly during the pandemic. Some of these women really committed to the exploration of the 12 Steps and dug deeply; some touched down and then disappeared; some merely attended; some rarely attended or dropped off altogether, just gone. I am all of those women at some level.

I could say working the Steps is hard, it requires a lot of showing up, digging in, being committed to self-investigation and learning to be kind about it. All of that is true. And, working the Steps is an ongoing process. It would not be kind or fair to myself to haul out all my habit patterns at once and attempt a full makeover of my behaviors. Working the Steps as I have, helped me learn to slow down, examine one pattern at a time. I learned to gently get to know myself. *Gently* allows what is hidden to come to the surface for full awareness. By the time my inner truth had finally emerged, changing my way of working with what I know was easier.

Continuing to work the Steps, to glean what I can from the process set forth in both the AA 12 Steps and the Proactive 12 Steps, is the best way to influence others to try them. I need not "proselytize" except by example. As part of the Al-Anon family groups, I have learned to fight the tendency to hide out in shame by being transparent. There is no one who cannot know that I am in "recovery" as the child of an alcoholic, and that I work the 12 Steps.

I have always likened inner work to that of archeology: a removal of the top crust of fear, anger, and bullshit; a more careful, precise removal of important artifacts in the underlayers; an uncovering of the *structure* that contained the artifacts; a standing back to see the whole picture (the dig site), and to seek from the evidence uncovered, a more thorough understanding of how I have been living. The only tool I need is the feather of awareness and curiosity, not the shovel of judgment.

Writing that contributed to *Sobering Thoughts*:

Drinking in America: Our Secret History by Susan Cheever, Twelve, New York, 2015.

Cheever's *Drinking in America* is a wonderful-horrible compendium of this nations' drinking history from the highest levels of society on down. This book illustrates the deep involvement of our citizenry with drinking right from the inception of our country, and how alcohol was as fundamental to the founding and flourishing of America as cotton and tobacco and politics. I quoted several passages.

Understanding the Alcoholic's Mind: The Nature of Craving and How to Control it by Arnold M. Ludwig, M.D., Oxford University Press, Oxford, 1988.

This book served as background for understanding the thinking process of alcoholics.

Terry Gorski, an internationally recognized expert on substance abuse and recovery and founder of *Cenaps,* an international organization providing advanced training in the field of behavioral health and addiction recovery.

I have quoted from Terry's wonderful article on healthy relationships.

"The Addicted Brain" by Fran Smith, National Geographic, 2017
Wonderful quotes about the dangers of drinking.

Colin Tipping, *Radical Forgiveness, Making Room for the Miracle,* audio book from Global 13 Productions, 1999; *www.radicalforgiveness.org.*

I reiterate Colin Tippings' Radical Forgiveness letter-writing exercise for its ability to help us see more deeply into difficult situations with people.

MADD (Mothers Against Drunk Driving) website, *www.madd.org* Some of the best "numbers" on alcohol and the effects on all levels of society.

Centers for Disease Control, *www.cdc.gov,* is cited for its stance on the *disease* of alcohol, for clarifying in no uncertain terms, the effects of alcoholism upon the whole person, and for statistics on alcoholic poisoning.

NIH National Institute on Alcohol Abuse and Alcoholism, *http://www.niaaa.nih.gov,* for the science, statistics and social ramifications of alcohol abuse in America.

Additional Citations

Dedication Page: "I have been in Sorrow's kitchen and licked out all the pots. Then I have stood on the peaky mountain wrapped in rainbows, with a harp and sword in my hands."
Zora Neale Hurston, from *Their Eyes Were Watching God, 1937, Lippincott*

Prologue: *"Abandon all hope, ye who enter here."* Dante, Inferno

Prologue: *Shamanic Mysteries of Egypt* by Linda Star-Wolf, 2007, Bear & Company

Prologue: *Shamanic Egyptian Astrology* by Linda Star-Wolf and Ruby Falconer, 2010, Bear & Company

Prologue: the Prayer of Saint Francis of Assisi: Wikipedia cites the founder of *La Ligue,* Father Esther Bouquerel, as the true author

Prologue: *When Things Fall Apart* by Pema Chodron, 1996, Shambhala

Chapter 1: "I was violating my standards faster than I could lower them," Robin Williams, on the Letterman show

Chapter 1: Elie Wiesel, "An abnormal response to an abnormal situation is normal."

Chapter 1: "Your earliest experiences teach you who you are." Helen Macdonald, author of *Hawk*

Chapter 1: *He who covers up his disease cannot expect to be cured.* African proverb, thought to be common in Burkina Faso

Chapter 1: "You have to have some reason to heal." Edgar Cayce

Chapter 1: Forgiveness: giving up the hope that the past could be different. Author unknown.

Chapter 2: *What the heart loves is the cure.* African proverb, attributed to the Dagara of Burkina Faso.

Chapter 2: *Drinking in America: Our Secret History,* by Susan Cheever, 2016, Twelve

Chapter 2: Christopher Hitchens on Kingsley Amos, also from Susan Cheever

Part II, Chapter 3: In the 1944 film "Gaslight" Charles Boyer plays the master manipulator of his young wife, played by Ingrid Bergman.

Chapter 3: Terry Gorski, founder of *Cenaps* and an internationally recognized expert on substance abuse and recovery, from "What Is A Healthy Relationship?" by Linda Atkins

Chapter 4: Insight Meditation, borrowing from Theravada Buddhism, Susan Salzberg

Chapter 5: The Serenity Prayer, from Alcoholics Anonymous, the big Blue Book, attributed to Rienhold Niebuhr, who attributes it to Friedrich Oetinger

Chapter 5: Radical Forgiveness writing exercise based on Colin Tipping's *Radical Forgiveness* book, 1998, Global Publishing

Chapter 5: The International Focusing Institute, *focusing.org,* founded by Eugene Gendlin, PhD

Part III Chapter 6: "The cure for loneliness is solitude." Marianne Moore, poet and writer

Chapter 6: Tony A's List, from Tony A's 12 Step Workbook, *https://freeaca908372589.files.wordpress.com/2021/07/tony-a-steps-work-book-copy.pdf*

Chapter 6: John O'Donohue, poet, 1997, Sounds True

Chapter 6: Nathaniel Hawthorne, *Rappaccini's Daughter*, 1844, short stories

Chapter 6: Carolyn North, The Experience of a Lifetime, 1998, Universe Publishing

Chapter 6: "The Addicted Brain" by Fran Smith, National Geographic, 2017

Chapter 6: Addendum, The 12 Steps and The Proactive 12 Steps by Serge Prengel, *Proactivechange.com*; His book, *The Proactive Twelve Steps: A Mindful Program for Lasting Change* by Serge Prengel, 6th edition, is available at Amazon via Active Pause press.

About Angel

I come from a long line of alcoholics, though I could never be one myself. I have often called myself a "cheap date." Though, in truth, I do not have a body that can hold enough addictive substance, then to want to do it again tomorrow and the next day, and so on.

From the time I was nearly 10, "magical" things have happened around me and to me. I have written about some of these events, because they are extraordinary, and because they immediately impressed me as evidence that there was much more to life than my family's dysfunction, or my suffering from abuse. I felt I was singled out for some good in life, not just for trauma. These events caused me to *wonder*, and wonder took me out of the mundane and into higher realms of awareness.

I have three kids, all grown, two married, one has two children. Though I never considered that I had enough good mothering to be a good mother, my kids are sane, funny, productive and smart.

When Bruce and I got married 3 years ago, two of my three kids joined us via Zoom, one from New York and one from New Orleans. The youngest is currently out of touch and I don't know why. I miss him.

My prior careers have been a non-denominational minister, bodyworker and Anatomy instructor, and before that, a house painter and baker.

In 2004, I published *Practically Perfect Wedding and Commitment Ceremonies* to help couples and officiators produce meaningful and personal wedding ceremonies; *Come to the Table*, a recollection of four generations of Weatherly women, their stories and recipes (out in 2024). *Stop Smoking Naturally*, through mindfulness practices in 2010; *The Wow and Oh-No of it*, an exploration of my cancer experience through prose and poetry in 2018; and The Art and Science of Healing, part memoir, part collaborative resource examining the healing arts through practice and case study, 2025. I maintain several blogs, help other writers, and post snarky-fun commentaries at the local online bulletin board under the pseudonym, Nosey Parker.

These days, Bruce and I tend our garden in west Sonoma County, where we maintain private practices coaching quantum leapers.

God, grant me the serenity
To accept the things I cannot change,
Courage to change the things I can,
And wisdom to know the difference.

Grant me patience
For the changes that take time.
An appreciation for all that I have.
Tolerance for those with different struggles,
And the strength to get up and try again,
One day at a time.